Life On Foot
A Walk Across America

Nate Damm

Not copyrighted, but if you use any material from this book, please attribute it to me or my website (natedamm.com) in some way. It's the nice thing to do.

Cover photo credit: Foster Huntington (arestlesstransplant.com)

~ For my parents and my brother ~

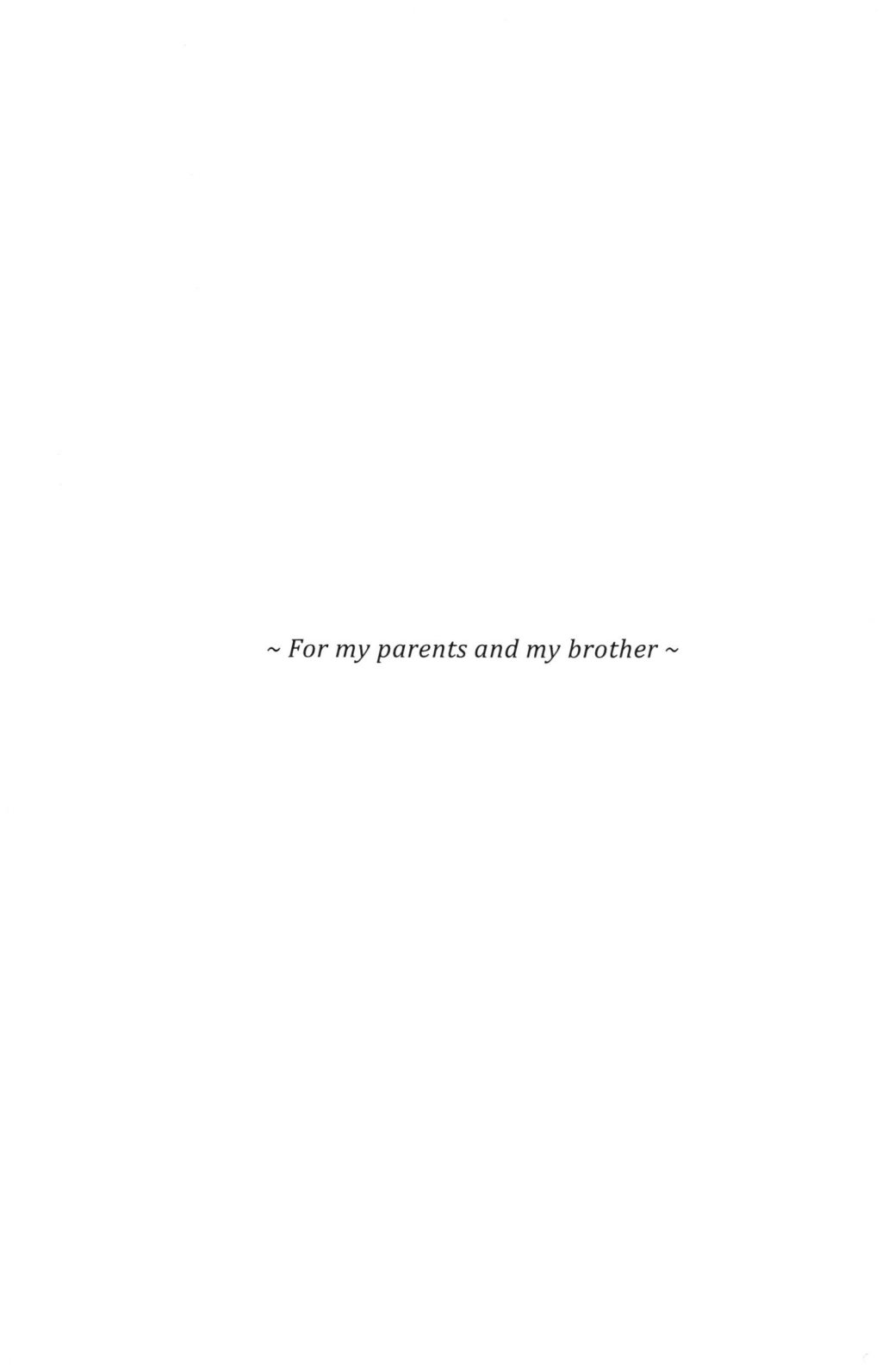

Chapter 1: An Idea

This story begins with an oil spill.
On January 19th, 1971, two oil tankers collided in San Francisco Bay, spilling over 800,000 gallons of crude oil into the bay area. The bay's contaminated water turned dark and glistened in the sunlight as the coastline and its residents, both human and animal, were bombarded by the contents of the disabled ships.

A young man named John Francis watched all of this unfold from a distance on that day. As the oil invaded the coastline, he saw the environment he loved so much suffer at the hands of the man-made disaster. Something changed in him. He watched and considered how his own actions had been responsible in a way for the travesty — the car he drove, the oil needed to transport the food he ate. He heard a man say over his vehicle's radio, "And if you don't like the news, go out and make some of your own."

Something in the man's words touched his soul and stuck in his mind like a catchy tune. Cleanup efforts were begun and finished, and the bay eventually went back to normal. Something inside of Francis refused to do the same.

It wasn't long before Francis decided to change the trajectory of his life and lessen his negative impact on the planet. He reflected on the spill and the inner turmoil that it, along with various other circumstances in his life, had brought about. Thinking of this, he made a decision that he had been considering for a while. He decided to stop using motorized transportation of any kind and begin living his life on foot. It was time to see what a slower pace could teach him.

Francis started walking, and did so exclusively for the next twenty-two years. For seventeen of those years, he also maintained a vow of silence. Francis walked across America, then the length of the South American continent while learning, listening to people, and inspiring others to live simply and in an environmentally friendly manner. In short, he had found what he was looking for, and he had found it through walking.

Sixteen years after John Francis began his travels, it was the summer of 1988. A wonderful year. He was busy making an impact on the world. I was busy being born. Fast forward another twenty years and that's where my story runs, or walks, face first into his.

~

It was sometime in 2008, can't remember which month. I was visiting my dad and step-mom at their house in Rangeley, Maine. As we chatted, I picked up an issue of *Backpacker Magazine* that sat on their coffee table to browse through. While scanning inattentively through its pages, an article caught my eye. I began to read it with half of my focus on the conversation with my parents and the other half on the page. After a few moments of reading, the voices around me had faded out.

Nothing against the conversation abilities of my parents, like any Mainers they are able to talk about everything and nothing in a stimulating fashion for hours, but the only person that mattered to me at that moment was a complete stranger. A man by the name of John Francis.

I finished reading the article that detailed his continent-spanning treks and many accomplishments, stood up from the couch, walked over to my parent's computer, fired up their archaic dial-up AOL Internet, waited for an absurd amount of time to get connected, and then began planning the rest of my life. Walking! This was it!

With the help of a Google search I found a trail called the American Discovery Trail that ran from coast to coast, and just like that, it was done. Leaning back in the squeaky office chair that my dad had been using for well over two decades, I said, "I think I'm going to walk across America."

~

Whether I fully realized it or not at the time, that article detailing John Francis' accomplishments had changed my life entirely. I had no idea that people walked across continents prior to reading it. It just wasn't a thing that people did. I knew about long distance trails like the Appalachian Trail and Pacific Crest Trail, but those were well-beaten paths surrounded by natural beauty. The concept of walking right out in the open on roads through cities and small towns from ocean to ocean had never so much as entered my mind for a moment. But once it did, I knew it was something I had to do.

Several months after reading the article in *Backpacker*, I was in a store browsing through a shelf of used books. Like most used bookshelves it contained a smattering of romance novels, monstrous photo books, and mediocre, ghost written celebrity memoirs. A quick glance down the shelf in search of something that wasn't complete crap revealed a choice that hadn't been returned to its designated slot after being pulled out by a shopper. It leaned haphazardly against the bindings of its fellow book orphans. Though I had no idea what the book was, something about it seemed familiar from a distance.

I walked over to it for a closer examination and discovered what I had recognized. The book's cover featured an image of a man walking down some railroad tracks with a big external frame backpack on his back. He was playing a banjo as he walked. I'd seen the man before. The title of the book was *Planetwalker*. It was the story John Francis had written about his twenty-two year journey on foot.

I grabbed the book off the shelf and stared at its cover for a few minutes. Never had an image of anything affected me so strongly. He looked so free, so happy, so at peace. Those were feelings I hadn't experienced in far too long. I took the book home and read it immediately, and it only solidified what I already knew. The walk was going to happen.

~

In February 2010, I was living in the small town of Winthrop, Maine. My girlfriend Alana and I were renting the upstairs of my mom's house and starting a nice little life together. She was finishing up her time in college, and I was working. We talked about how we would get married someday. We had a dog. We were doing what young people who love each other do.

On one of these blistering cold February afternoons in Maine, the idea of walking across America was bothering me more than usual. It simply refused to quit, and was becoming downright disruptive as it permeated into every aspect of my existence. I couldn't focus on anything. It consumed me. It was on that day that I decided enough was enough.

I promised myself that if July rolled around and the idea was still something that I was interested in pursuing, I was going to commit to the walk and start planning it. It's funny how we try to control things we know we really can't by setting ultimatums and schedules. Deep down I knew I was still going to want to do it in six months, regardless of the circumstances.

Later on that day, Alana returned home from class and we were relaxing and watching some TV. I turned to her and said, "What do you think about me walking across America for eight or nine months? Would you be cool with that?" I was nervous to ask her about it. Like she would just pack up her things, grab the dog, and never be heard from again just because I brought it up. I hadn't talked about it with her much at all before that point, mainly because I figured that the novelty of the idea would just wear off. At the time, I was the kind of person who got big, exciting ideas and started making outlandish plans to make them happen, only to then struggle to bring them to fruition due to a waning attention span and a set of interests resembling something like a revolving door. I was really all over the place, and knew it well. This contributed to my hesitancy to speak about what I had been brooding over.

But on that day I brought it up. After telling her that I was actually getting serious about the idea and asking if she thought it was a good thing to do, Alana turned, looked at me, and said with a smile, "Yeah, if that's what you want to do." I could have said I wanted to build my own spaceship in the garage and go to the moon and she would have supported me. I don't know why I was so nervous to ask.

We talked about it for another minute or so before the subject changed to something else. But my mind was still on that idea. That seemingly impossible and far off idea.

~

By July, Alana and I had moved into a place of our own in Rangeley, the same town where my dad and step-mom lived. Most of her family lived there as well. I was working for her parents at the marina and convenience store they owned on Rangeley Lake. I handled boat rentals, cleaned boats, and did all sorts of other odd jobs there. It was probably the only job I had ever really enjoyed going to every day.

I thought of Alana's step-dad as a sort of mentor. I had virtually no experience in anything that I was responsible for doing at work, but he hired me anyway. My tasks included driving four wheelers (barely done before), backing up boat trailers (never done before), painting (done!), cleaning boats (never done before), doing small carpentry jobs (never done before), and driving boats (never done before). He was a patient and talented teacher, and eventually I got the hang of a few things. I gained a lot of new skills and knowledge working there. The rest of Alana's family was great, as well, and welcomed me in like I had just always been around.

Life was good. I'd happily return home from my daily adventures at work to Alana and our pets, and had every reason in the world to be completely content. For the most part, I was. But a nagging feeling I had just wouldn't go away. A longing for some adventure, jitters from the realization that I was settling down a bit, I didn't know.

~

I kept my self-made promise and committed to walking across America in July. I decided to start walking in March. Alana seemed to be behind the idea, and my parents showed me nothing but support. Many of my friends didn't seem to believe that I was going to do it, but that was probably because I didn't talk about it much unless I had consumed a few beers. It was just drunk talk as far as they were concerned.

Most nights I would go outside onto the porch of the house that Alana and I lived in and think about the walk. We lived in the western mountains of Maine. Towering pines surrounded my evening place of solitude and thought. I would sit there under the stars, smoke a cigar, watch the moon. This was where I wondered about things. Something in the night sky would ignite my sense of adventure. I'd want to take off right that minute. High aspirations for a small town kid who had never been west of Pennsylvania. I'd feel buzzed on thoughts of the walk, then go back inside and see Alana and our dog and instantly know I would miss them. I became more and more sad each day as a result of this back and forth routine. My soul was pulling me in two opposite directions.

All this confusion caused me to grow distant and withdrawn. Alana, my best friend in the world, seemed to take the brunt of the consequences that came along with it. I began questioning things I'd never questioned before, and she noticed the effect it had on me. With my attention and desires being stretched out to the point that I didn't seem to know anything anymore, I became less invested in what we had been building together for over two years. I was part of a team, but wasn't pulling my own weight. I felt awful for wanting something more than what I already had. At the end of the day, I knew that it was ideal.

In December, just a few months before I was set to begin the walk, Alana and I finally had a talk that we both knew was coming. We understood that we wanted different things, but were both trying to push through anyway. She wanted to settle into a more normal existence that included a home, kids, and that sort of stuff. I just wanted to walk, alone. Those real-life things could come at some point, but I didn't even want to think about them until the walk was over. I was feeling an overwhelming sense of guilt about leaving her to hit the road, which would force her to put off her dreams until I was ready to be a part of them.

It was a chilly, snowy night when we talked about everything and I packed my things into my car and left. Before pulling out of our driveway, I took one last look at the house. I could see Alana crying through a window. Our dog had his front paws up on that same window and peered out at me. He looked like he knew I wouldn't be back again.

~

I had just lost my best friend, dog, cat, apartment, and job in a single conversation. A couple days later, my friend told me that my life had turned into a sad country song. It really had.

This began the most heartbreaking and difficult time I had experienced in my life up to that point. I went into hiding and ended up staying in the spare room at my mom's house, while trying to endure the handful of drawn-out days that still had to ever so slowly play out before the walk would start. I didn't really have anywhere else to go. No one even knew that Alana and I had split up for at least a week. I didn't want to talk to anyone. Just being alive was almost unbearable. I didn't just think that I had made the biggest mistake of my life, I knew it.

There was nothing to do except wait, and when the time came (believe me it came slowly), to walk. In the meantime, I went into self-destruct mode. Lots of drinking and long nights followed. I barely slept for days on end. I remember sitting around one afternoon watching TV and drinking rum right out of the bottle. I was a real piece of shit. I tried to stay busy, but there was nobody to do anything with. My friends spent their days working like productive, normal people and didn't have time for someone as pathetic as me. For some reason, shoveling the snow outside of the house helped me feel a bit better, so I shoveled a lot of snow. Thankfully, it snowed a lot that winter. I sunk lower and lower to a place that I'd never been before, one where I felt suffocated and trapped.

Looking back now, there was a bit of light at the end of the tunnel, after all. At one time or another, we have all thought about the one thing that we believe could be the key to our happiness. We think: *If I could only get/have _____, things would be much better.* This almost never works out as we hope it will.

Walking was what I would put in that blank, and it was one of the rare cases where the blank was right. Walking would save me.

Chapter 2: A Fresh Start

On February 25th, 2011, my mother drove me from Maine to Delaware, and we stayed at a motel near the beach at Cape Henlopen State Park, where I was set to begin my trek. Gusts flew off the Atlantic and pummeled the side of the building. The entire place creaked and seemed to move with each blow.

I wasn't supposed to start walking until March 1st, but my restlessness got the best of me soon after we arrived at the motel. I decided I'd begin the next morning, February 26th. I didn't sleep much that night, but it wasn't due to fear or nervousness. I was just lost in contemplative thought. All of the things that had led me up to that moment ran through my head. I saw Alana and our apartment, her family, my family. I saw the image of John Francis with his banjo marching down those railroad tracks.

As I laid in bed and the wind slammed against the motel and howled outside, I thought about the fact that the next night I would probably be camping in such conditions. It would be cold and terrifying. I settled on the idea that I deserved whatever hardship awaited me down the road. I was a selfish, foolish person. Facing problems head-on instead of hiding from them in a bottle or a bed would be the best thing for me.

Eventually I dozed off, and in the morning I felt energized as my mother and I made our way to the state park, where we found the beginning of the American Discovery Trail. It was time.

A wave of relaxation came over me as we pulled into the beach parking lot. All I had to do at that point was walk. No more planning, no more questioning whether or not I was doing the right thing. Just walk. That's it. There was no turning back, and I liked it.

My mom left me for a few minutes on the beach to be alone. She sensed that I needed some space. It was just me and Wilson there. Wilson was the name of my backpack. He was named after Tom Hanks' character's volleyball in the movie *Castaway*. The volleyball was his only friend on a deserted island, Wilson would be my only friend on deserted highways. The name seemed appropriate. Wilson is the true star of this book.

    I took out my camera to record a video on the beach. Muttering out a few mindless sentences, I took the first steps of my walk on camera, then made my way up the beach to the parking lot where my mom was waiting. Her eyes welled up and she hugged me goodbye, then she drove away. Stinging tears blurred my vision as her car disappeared around a corner. No son likes to see his mom cry.

    And just like that, I was alone. I stepped onto a trail that led out of the state park — sun, fragrant pine trees, cool ocean breeze. A fresh start.

~

    In the early afternoon on that first day of walking in Delaware, a big four-door truck stopped at an intersection ahead of me as I approached the town of Milton. I thought that it was sitting there for a strangely long amount of time, and figured out why as I approached the truck and its window rolled down. A man, who was probably in his 30s, leaned out the window and yelled, "WHAT ARE YOU DOING WITH YOUR LIFE?" at me loudly as the truck sped off.

    I remember thinking that it was a very valid question.

    I stopped at the Milton Police Department, where I was quite rudely rejected by an officer when I inquired about camping in the town park. With that plan shut down, the only option I had was to keep moving.

As I was leaving town in search of a hidden patch of woods to camp in, I noticed a family coming toward me on the sidewalk. There was a man, woman, and two young girls on bikes. One of the girls lost control of her steering bar and took a hard fall just ahead. I approached the scene of the accident and asked the man if she was ok. He smiled and said that she was fine, then asked what I was up to. I told him.

His eyes lit up instantly when I explained what I was doing. I had a hunch that my day was about to get a lot better. He asked where I was planning on sleeping for the night, and I told him that I didn't have a clue. "Well, you're welcome to camp in our backyard if you want," he said as the rest of the family nodded along in agreement.

I replied with an emphatic "Ok!" then walked up several beautiful streets to their home, but lagged back a bit from the group on account of my swollen feet. The girls raced and swerved around on their bikes ahead as I limped around in the background. We arrived shortly and I set my tent up for the first time on their spacious lawn.

The man's name was Jeremy. He suggested that we walk up to the Dog Fish Head brewery that was near his house. All I heard him say was the word brewery and agreed that it sounded like a good idea. I tried to act like I knew what I was talking about while answering all of his questions about the trip as we walked there, and wondered if he could tell that I actually didn't know anything at all. We walked into the main building of the brewery and Jeremy immediately told the people working there what I was doing. Thanks to his promotion, I landed a free beer. Eight hours into the walk and I was already drinking, and shortly thereafter, smoking.

One of the very few goals I had for the walk was to not smoke. No cigars, no cigarettes, no other stuff that people smoke. I had never been what I would consider a big smoker, but I did enjoy some tobacco products from time to time. I felt that a walk across the country would be a fitting opportunity to give them up completely. But Jeremy had some high quality tobacco that he was telling me about, which he seemed to be longing to get into. He was currently in the process of quitting smoking and perhaps looking for a reason to have a bit of a relapse, so he asked me if I wanted to smoke a cigarette. I'm sure that in his mind, he used the excuse that it would be rude not to make such an offer to a guest, then join if I accepted it. I used the excuse that it was an offer from a host, and that it would be rude to refuse it as a guest. We used each other perfectly.

Jeremy and I spent the rest of the evening sitting by a fire, smoking hand rolled cigarettes, and enjoying a couple beers. Overall, things seemed like they were getting off on the right foot.

The next morning, I woke up, took a shower, and was ready to hit the road early. Jeremy was going to walk with me for part of the morning. My feet were in miserable shape, so I wasn't in any sort of hurry anyway, which ended up being good thing, because Jeremy had a stop in mind for our trip out of a still sleepy downtown Milton.

This stop was at a Christian church in town, where he wanted the pastor to pray a blessing over me. Arriving at the church, we met with the pastor — a sincere, soft-spoken man — in his small office. He placed his hand on my shoulder and prayed out loud for me. After the prayer, Jeremy and I headed out of town toward Redden State Forest. Traffic was slow, a welcomed relief, and so was our progress thanks to steady conversation and my battered feet. After a couple of miles of talking and swapping stories, which was so enjoyable that I actually forgot about the jabbing needle sensation that shot through my body with each step for a few blissful moments, I found myself alone once again as Jeremy headed back to his wife and kids.

Not long after Jeremy turned back I sat down, removed my shoes and socks, and began the tedious work that was tending to my blisters. Things were popping and gushing everywhere. I tried to clean and bandage them as well as I could. My feet shouted out their displeasure with sharp stabs of pain. I managed to stand up and keep trudging onward after a while, like I would do thousands more times before I reached the other ocean. After all, there was really nothing else to do.

Later on in the afternoon after the blister popping party, I was slowly hobbling down a secluded road when a truck pulled up next to me. The lady who was driving it asked, "When did you start?" out the rolled down window.

Her question caught me off guard. She appeared to know what I was doing. Nobody I'd met seemed to know that the American Discovery Trail even existed, despite it crossing right through their own neighborhoods. I replied, "I'm hiking on the American Discovery Trail, walking across America."

"I know," she said sarcastically.

"You know? Nobody around here seems to know the trail is even here," I said.

She smiled and said, "I'm Serinda, my husband's name is Reese. We've hosted a few ADT hikers. Give me your phone number. I'll call you later today and find out where you ended up. If you want, you can come stay with us."

Serinda was organized and to the point. It clearly wasn't her first time dealing with an overwhelmed and under-experienced hiker. I wrote down my phone number and tried not-so-successfully to hide the smile that was begging to take over my face. I sat down on a small embankment to eat an orange as Serinda drove off. Looking up at the cloudless sky, I thought to myself that maybe everything was going to be ok after all.

~

It wasn't too long before I called Serinda and she made the drive out to get me. She told me about her husband, Reese, and their three kids, Ethan, Cyrus, and Lydia, on the drive to their home. Goose was on the menu for dinner, and I could sleep in the living room next to a warm fireplace. I felt like I'd just won the hobo lottery. We arrived at the house, and after a much-appreciated hot shower and a filling dinner, we all watched a documentary about hiking the Appalachian Trail and ate ice cream. I couldn't have imagined a better second night on the road.

The next day I attempted to walk in the rain. It was a disaster. My feet were already blistered, so once they got wet and rubbed against the insides of my boots, large sections of my skin began sliding off. I was shivering and pacing back and forth next to a corn field to stave off hypothermia when Reese showed up in the late afternoon to rescue me. I had learned a valuable lesson early on — there is really no way to stay dry except by getting the hell out of the rain. Riding back to the house, I could only think about how happy I was that I would get to sleep by the crackling fire again.

Reese and Serinda were top-notch parents. Their household had a well-mannered, yet still fun and silly atmosphere about it. Lydia, Cyrus, and Ethan were as good as kids get. I was feeling pretty lonely at the time and still reeling from my entire life falling out from under me, so being with a family brought me a certain level of comfort that I desperately needed. I ended up staying with the Conner family for two days. After cherishing a couple days of comfort, I headed out on my own again into the Delaware countryside.

~

I noticed something interesting as I was walking into and through the tiny town of Bridgeville, Delaware. People in Delaware, particularly older men, enjoyed sitting in their garages for long periods of time. A garage in Delaware is often not used for vehicle storage of any kind. It is a place where men can be men and enjoy a cheap domestic beer and conversation while surrounded by power tools, old engine parts, and outdated calendars with busty women on them.

I was walking by one of these garage hangouts when I heard a call from inside, "Hey, where ya headed?"

I said, "I'm walking across the U.S. to California."

"Well get over here and grab a drink and take a seat," the man inside said.

This is how I met Mark and Bill.

Mark appeared to be in his mid-to-late sixties, Bill in his fifties. Mark seemed to be almost completely blind. I would later learn that he nearly was. He had a smile on his face all the time. I'm not sure if he was really smiling or just squinting to try to see better, but either way, he was a happy man. Bill was quiet, had a blackish gray beard, and wore thick glasses. Mark and Bill were best buddies.

There was a labyrinth of equipment in every stage of disrepair imaginable on the lawn in front of the garage. We sat at a long, foldable table inside the garage that was covered in packaging for various mechanical parts, a can of Rust-Oleum, and a few other miscellaneous items. The table's seats were old van or truck seats that had been removed from their original vehicles and placed around it.

Mark grabbed me a can of Mountain Dew and a cold beer for himself from a refrigerator. Bill had quit drinking a while back and shared the fact with pride. Mark slowly opened his bottle of Corona, put the cap down on the table, and just stared at it for a while in silence. I looked at him for a moment as he did this. He could tell I was confused. He said, "My wife, who's now passed away, had a rule. No drinking until noon. So I make sure to still follow it."

I glanced at my cell phone. It was 11:50 AM and he was going to wait the ten minutes. That was true love if I had ever seen it.

Mark gave me his address when I finished my Mountain Dew and was ready to get back on the road. "Send me a postcard from San Francisco," he said. I promised I would. It felt good that upon giving me a close examination in the form of many questions and some manly garage hang out time, he thought I might actually make it there.

About a month later, a friend of mine, Tyler Coulson, started his own journey across America on foot. He mentioned hanging out with a couple of older guys in a garage in Delaware when we talked on the phone about a week into his trip. I knew it had to have been Mark and Bill, and it sure was.

I ambled down a dirt road after leaving the garage. Quiet fields of dull brown grass tried desperately to escape from the last grip of winter. The path followed a ditch filled with what had to have been at least fifty rotting deer carcasses. A deer graveyard was the last thing I remember seeing in Delaware.

Chapter 3: Cities

On March 1st, I walked over the Mason-Dixon Line and into the second state of my traverse, Maryland. This historic division of land was, and to many still is, the unofficial line dividing the American North and South.

I walked slowly down winding back roads, some of them without a center line. The open farmland soothed my mind as my feet, back, and shoulders begged for a break. The landscape was mostly brown with hints of green in places. Hundreds of Snow Geese spent their days whining loudly about something while congregating in the wide fields. I could feel spring coming and couldn't wait for its arrival. The mornings when I had to get out of my warm sleeping bag and emerge into freezing temperatures were a bit frosty for my liking.

I spent a couple nights getting my first taste of trespassing while camping illegally in closed state parks. Both times, park rangers drove by in the morning, looked at me, and drove off without a word. That was when I realized that park rangers probably didn't get paid enough to really care about traveling kids like me.

The days passed quickly, but the nights were not as cooperative. My mind was in the process of adjusting to the road. The realization that there was very little I could actually control in my new existence was hitting me hard. Putting one foot in front of the other was about the only thing I had a say in. This kept me up, tossing and turning for a solution.

~

I soon found myself in Queenstown, Maryland with dark fast approaching. There I crossed US Route 50 for the first time, a multiple-lane monstrosity with heavy traffic. It was my initial encounter with the road that would be my home for many of the coming months.

The area was densely populated and there was a large outlet mall nearby, so finding a place to sleep was proving to be problematic. After grabbing a slice of pizza at a local pizzeria, I called a couple of churches for help with a resting spot, but nobody answered. I then went to the local town office, but nobody there was of any assistance. I decided to just make my way out of town and hope something would present itself.

Soon after, I walked by an American Legion building, Post 296. I continued on past it for a few minutes. For some reason, I ended up settling on the idea to turn around and go back to ask if I could camp on the property behind Legion building. I was scared to death, as it would be my first cold call, but it had to be done.

Approaching the door slowly with my heart about to explode out of my chest, I reached for the handle and turned it. Locked. The door handle made a clicking noise when I turned it, which somehow managed to attract the attention of everyone in the place, despite the steady clamor of buzzed conversation and music. There were a few awkward moments when I could see people sitting inside at the bar looking at me, looking at each other, and saying, "Who the hell is that homeless guy at the door?"

After what seemed like minutes of this, a guy stood up from his place at the bar and came to the door. I nervously said, "My name is Nate Damm. I'm walking across the country and just happened to be passing by. Was wondering if there is any chance I could set my tent up on the lawn behind your building to get some sleep for the night."

The man said, "I don't see why not, but come on in and we'll make sure."

I repeated myself to someone behind the bar, and they confirmed that it was fine. All was going smoothly until I heard an old lady down the bar say loudly, "Well, I wouldn't let him stay on my property, that's for sure," and storm off. She knew I could hear every word she said. She apparently had some sort of authority there, so her strong disapproval of the idea made me nervous. I could already see myself huddling up under the awning of one of the high class outlet stores up the road and being forced to leave in the middle of the night by the police. My fears were quickly diminished, however, when the three guys sitting closest to where I was standing at the bar started laughing uproariously. They told me to ignore her, and that she was just a bitter old broad. They promptly handed me a can of Budweiser and said I was more than welcome to go get everything set up out back.

After thanking them about ten times, I walked back behind the building to set up my tent, then recorded a video for my website. A delicious dinner of nearly frozen ravioli right out of the can was prepared. As I was about to dig in, I heard someone calling to me from the building. "Hey man! Get in here and have a beer!"

I crawled out of my home and sprayed smelly boots with Odor Eaters. After hobbling my way over to the building on blistered feet, I took a much needed seat at the bar with the boys. Things became fun from that point on. Maybe a little too fun. My three buddies at the bar were pretty intent on getting me intoxicated and feeding me as much food as they could.

During this memorable display of American hospitality, I ended up drinking nine beers and eating most of an entire pizza. I felt fat and satisfied as I stumbled in a drunken haze back to my tent to prepare for a cold night of sleep, several hours after I walked into the friendliest bar in Queenstown.

~

The next morning, I broke down my camp, and my hands went numb from the frost that had formed on the outside of my tent overnight. Severely hungover and cold, I longed to get on the pavement so the early morning sun could warm me up a bit.

I hopped on the Cross Island Trail after crossing the Kent Narrows drawbridge. The trail and surrounding roads meandered through pine forests coated with leaves from the previous fall until reaching Chesapeake Bay with its open marshes and marinas lined with sailboats and small fishing vessels. At the end of the trail I met up with Mike, an American Discovery Trail volunteer who regularly assisted hikers with a ride across the Chesapeake Bay Bridge. The bridge is illegal for pedestrians to cross. I enjoyed having a conversation partner as I gazed out over the bay, still in disbelief that I was actually on the trip I had dreamed about for so long. I was overwhelmingly homesick, but for some reason it felt fine as we rolled across the bridge.

Mike drove an old gray Mercedes that oozed with character. It had made a cross-country trip of its own the previous year on the famed Lincoln Highway. I would later walk many of the roads that Mike and his beloved Mercedes rambled down. We drove into Annapolis and saw the prestigious grounds of the United States Naval Academy. Narrow streets initially constructed for horses and carriages led us down toward the waterfront and the most historic district of the city. We passed the Maryland State House. It served as the home of the United States government when Annapolis was the capital of the nation for just under a year in the early 1780s.

After a delicious lunch, which included some locally harvested crab, we took a stroll around historic Annapolis in the City Dock area. Many of the area's buildings were still in their original state, looking nearly exactly as they did during the mid-1700s. They were surrounded by shops of all types and sat alongside a marina filled with million dollar yachts. It was a rather charming blend of old and new, for the most part. As we walked, Mark filled me in on a particularly interesting controversy that had taken place a few years earlier regarding a nearby building in Annapolis.

The King Of France Tavern opened for business in 1784, when Annapolis was the capital of the still under a decade old United States. It was one of the more popular local hangouts for politicians, including many of the men we now recognize as the Founding Fathers. Local legend even claims that George Washington lost a horse in a card game there. What an amazing piece of history to preserve for years to come, right?

I guess not. Since 2007, the famed location on historic Church Street has been a Starbucks. The local watering hole where our earliest leaders would get drunk and lose horses in card games had been turned into a place of overpriced lattes and hipster baristas.

I felt angry when I heard this. Many locals had the same reaction. It was the first of many instances I saw on the walk where a priceless historical landmark was destroyed for the sake of commerce or convenience.

Life On Foot

~

The next day of walking took me into the city of Bowie. The sun was nearly setting as I arrived, and I seemed to be making a habit of walking myself into bad situations when it came to finding a place to rest.

I crossed the bustling monster known as US Route 301 and plopped myself down at a McDonald's soon after entering the city. With my laptop out, I decided to check out Couchsurfing.org to see if there were any hosts available in the area. It would be unlikely on such incredibly short notice.

I found one profile that looked promising, created an account of my own (didn't even have one yet), and sent the guy a message. It basically said that I knew it was a long shot, but I was walking across the country, was badly unprepared, and didn't have a place to stay that very night. I included my phone number in the message and doubted that the guy would actually call. Leaving McDonald's, I headed out through a shopping mall, crossed an awful graffiti covered footbridge over a highway, then just kept on walking without much of an idea as to where I was actually going.

As Bowie was in the process of swallowing me whole, my phone rang. To my pleasant surprise, it was the Couchsurfing guy, Ben. It couldn't have been more than half an hour since I had left the McDonald's. He said to meet him up ahead at the Benjamin Tasker Middle School, where he would pick me up shortly. I was welcome to stay in the guest room at his house. In my mind at that moment, a miracle had just occurred on the streets of Bowie.

It didn't take much time to get to the school. I waited there for a bit while trying not to look like the creepy guy who stands outside a middle school for no apparent reason. Ben showed up after not too long. As I was loading my stuff into the trunk of his car, he asked, "Do you know anything about this school?"

"Nope, I don't," I said.

He informed me that it was the school where the Beltway snipers, John Allen Muhammad and Lee Boyd Malvo, had stopped focusing on adults and shot their first child victim back in October of 2002. Iran Brown, who was 13 at the time, was shot not far from where Ben and I were standing as he arrived at school. Ben then showed me the upper parking lot where Muhammad and Malvo had parked their vehicle and chosen Brown as their target. Brown ended up surviving his injuries and testifying against Muhammad at his trial. I clearly remembered seeing the ordeal on the news when it happened years earlier.

It was a short drive to the house where Ben lived with his wife, Allison. I became even more amazed at my good fortune when I figured out that they lived only about a block from the road I was supposed to begin walking on the following day.

Ben and Allison's house was immaculate. I quickly made myself at home in a nicely decorated and spacious upstairs bedroom. After a shower I joined them downstairs for pizza and a movie. Not even an hour earlier I was lost and scared. Now here I was, in what seemed like the blink of an eye, freshly showered, eating pizza, and watching a movie in someone's home. I was learning that the experience of the road is one typically made up of soaring highs and rock-bottom lows, and that they often occur in rapid succession.

~

Leaving Ben and Allison's home in the morning, I disappeared from the cramped neighborhoods of Bowie and found myself back in quiet pastureland. I walked past massive plots of government owned land. Every 100 feet or so there were signs that read: NO TRESPASSING - U.S. GOVERNMENT PROPERTY. The signs made me uneasy.

One of the signs was so weathered that it just said "NO." I yelled "YES!" at it loudly and proceeded along my way. I wondered about how crazy I would be by California if I was already yelling at signs in Maryland. There was so much to look forward to.

The next city I hit was College Park, where I walked straight through an area of low-income housing projects. Nothing against low-income folks, I am one myself at the moment, but it's not exactly a secret that low-income government housing tends to mean high crime rates. I took in scenery such as homeless gentlemen drinking beers out of paper bags at 10 AM and all the graffiti I could ever hope to look at.

From there the day would only get worse. Following the Greenbelt Lake Trail for a while past public playgrounds and old men spending their days fishing, I entered Greenbelt Park.

Greenbelt Park was awful. Signage for roads, trails, and camping areas were very unclear, if present at all. I was trying to make my way through the park to get to the College Park Metro Station, where I could take the Metro to Fairfax, Virginia. My brother lived there, and I would be taking a few days off at his place.

Out of nowhere the weather turned poor, which only added to my disorientation. Things began to get ugly. Torrential rain poured down as I tried to follow a trail to the road I was supposed to be on. It ended up being a loop back to where I had started. I walked about a mile to a ranger station, was given vague directions, and ended up back at the station within an hour, thoroughly soaked and chilled to the bone. Just prior to this I talked to a young couple at a parking area, who told me how to get where they thought I needed to go. Of course, they were wrong. Wasted energy, miles, and time accumulated at an alarming rate.

I don't know how much time I spent in the black hole that was Greenbelt Park, but it was much too long. Finally, after my second round of directions from a park ranger and making sure he was extremely specific (you have to be when there are no signs), I made it out of the vortex and back into civilization. A short walk later, in the still pouring rain, I was at the Metro station on the verge of exploding with frustration and ready for the lengthy ride to Fairfax.

Things started to get dangerous when I noticed I was still shivering uncontrollably even after I had gotten onto the Metro train and been out of the rain for at least forty-five minutes. I could not for the life of me get close to warm. My thoughts were turning fuzzy and I was exhausted to the point that I could barely move at all.

I sent a message to my brother, Ezra, and told him to have the heat on in his car as high as possible for my upcoming arrival at the Fairfax station. Rapidly approaching a hypothermic situation, I heaved myself into his Ford Taurus and removed as much of my damp clothing as I could. The heat blasted out of the vents as we drove off, and I began to slowly warm up on the drive. The shivering had stopped by the time we reached his house. What a day.

For the next five days I took some much needed recovery time at Ezra's. My feet healed up a bit and my body regained some lost strength. Then I reversed all that good progress in a few nights of drinking. Regardless, I was ready to get back on the road after my time there. Or should I say, trail.

Chapter 4: The C&O

Ahead of me was a part of the walk I had been looking forward to with a giddy sort of excitement, the C&O Canal towpath. The C&O towpath trail follows the route of the historic Chesapeake and Ohio Canal. The canal was used from 1831 to 1924, serving as a major vein of economic growth and commerce along the Potomac River between Washington D.C. and Cumberland, Maryland. Today, the old towpath that was once used by mules to pull barges down the canal is a well-maintained trail used by walkers and bicyclists. There are free camping areas, outhouses, and drinking water pumps placed roughly every five miles along its length.

After walking down the cobbled streets of Georgetown, I arrived at the wooden sign that announced the beginning of the trail. I snapped a photo and was off. A drunken homeless fellow wandered by me while shouting loudly to himself as I took my first few steps on the path. He was one last reminder that I was ready to get the hell out of the city.

I spoke with my dad about the C&O while at Ezra's house in Fairfax, and even went so far as to say that it was a "hiker's heaven." I envisioned long mileage each day, water bottles constantly filled with water from perfectly placed pumps, and clear paths all the way to Cumberland. It was going to be marvelous. And I'm sure it would have been. But it was March. Dreary, cold March.

It turned out that the Potomac River was a magnet for the snowmelt that poured out of the mountains of Virginia, West Virginia, and anywhere else snow fell in the area. Because of this, it swells to about double its normal size every spring. This was actually a pivotal reason for the closing of the C&O in 1924. Floods nearly destroyed it far too often for it to be a sound investment any longer.

As I got a bit further down the C&O, it also became apparent that the National Park Service turned off the water pumps along the trail during the winter and didn't turn them back on until mid-April. Just a couple of days earlier I had called the towpath a "hiker's heaven." I wanted to kick myself in the mouth.

Within the first half hour of walking on the path out of the city, I found myself in a relatively quiet forest. Despite the trail not being exactly what I thought it would be, it was refreshing to be amongst nature with no cars, drunken people, and graffiti to distract me. It felt like a true escape. Birds fluttered by while singing in celebration of the oncoming spring. The crunching of my feet on the gravel eased my nerves, which had been jolted by the city and its business.

I got my first glimpse into how insane the flooding could, and had, become in the area at Great Falls, a popular place for tourists to come and gawk at the Potomac and get a sense of its power. The churning river was an impressive sight. The dark gray sky above made it appear even more ominous than it already was. I stood near the railing of a concrete observation area and watched the swollen mass of Appalachian snowmelt. It carried entire trees and other assorted debris downriver with ease. Frigid water rushed over areas of land that were usually dry riverbank. It was a chaotic frenzy that roared and took over.

A couple miles down the trail, I found the campsite that was my end destination for the day. It was under five feet of water when I arrived. The outhouse facility just beyond it was almost completely submerged. There was a narrow footbridge over the canal there, so I crossed it and put my tent up on the other side of the great ditch. There was a flat and dry spot next to one of the canal's many old lockhouses. Lockhouses were the buildings that once housed the men who monitored the locks along the canal, along with their families. Being on the other side of the canal created a convenient barrier between the unpredictable water level and myself.

I was almost certain the lockhouse was haunted. It looked eerie in the dim, freezing evening. Once it was set up, I crawled inside my little nylon home to call Alana and tell her I missed her. She didn't seem to care at all. I told her that I wished she would wait for me to get home so we could be together again. She said she didn't want to. I didn't blame her one bit. I knew that I would get this answer from her, but I felt like asking anyway, mostly out of homesick desperation.

Bringing such a thing up on a frosty night in a lonely and potentially haunted place was probably not the best idea. I was haunted enough by my own decisions. I didn't need actual ghosts crashing my pity party for one. A rush of cold wind shook the walls of my tent as I turned off my phone and hunkered down for another night of fitful sleep.

~

Most of the next day was spent dealing with flood waters that had overtaken the trail. I had the choice to either leave the C&O and take a mile-heavy route around the flooding or suck it up and slog through. I chose to slog. Removing my boots, I slung them over my shoulder and waded through the numbing waters. The most demanding stretch of flooded trail was well over half a mile long. The water level was over my knees and had a steadily pulling current. I aimed between the trees that lined the buried trail. Slipping down its slanted sides into the river to my left or the canal to my right could have been disastrous. The combination of the swiftly moving water and Wilson's weight would drag me down into the murky depths in no time should my footing be lost.

Stepping cautiously, I slowly made my way back to dry ground after 20 minutes or so. I put my socks and boots back on my feet, which were completely numb from the 40 degree water. I rounded the path's next corner, focused on moving quickly to warm up, only to witness another expanse of flooded trail ahead. I sighed, removed my boots, and waded into the biting current once more.

~

Approaching Harpers Ferry, West Virginia on the C&O, I passed a turn off for the Appalachian Trail. It headed northbound to Maine and southbound to Georgia. I stood at the intersection and thought about home. It was about 1,000 miles away, but seemed so much closer. I knew if I set foot on the northbound trail and kept walking, I could hike directly home to Rangeley. That would be it. I could be back quickly enough to possibly salvage the life I had given up. I sat down on the ground and stared at the path for a while.

After pondering this for a bit, I stood up and continued westbound, not northbound. I did my best to smile through the pain of knowing that things would never be the same again, and marched toward the setting sun that was dipping below the leafless trees that surrounded me. Turning around, I saw my shadow casting out to the east — a reminder of the old me and the stationary way of living I had given up. Movement had become life. It had to.

Crossing the still exploding Potomac on a footbridge, I found myself on a nearly noiseless Harpers Ferry street lined with shops, museums, and inns. Harpers Ferry was a quaint little community and still looked as it did during the mid-to-late 1800s. The town had been chosen by George Washington (that guy who lost his horse in a card game at the Starbucks in Annapolis) to house a military arsenal in 1794. In 1859, when abolitionist John Brown was at the height of his desperate campaign to lead a rebellion, the arsenal just happened to still be there. Brown had the bright idea to overtake the arsenal, and to begin his rebellion with its contents by distributing weapons to slaves and abolitionists throughout The South. Things didn't quite go as he had planned. The operation turned into a bloody mess, and most of Brown's fellow raiders ended up killed or captured. Several residents of Harpers Ferry also lost their lives in the struggle. Brown himself was captured and hung to death.

As you could imagine, Harpers Ferry was absolutely loaded with John Brown related stuff. There was a wax museum that looked interesting, but I didn't want to spend the money on its entrance fee. I peeked in the window and could see an eerily lifelike figure of John Brown, giving me the type of fiercely determined glare I would expect from someone who had the idea to break into a federal arsenal to start a rebellion. A worthy cause, for sure, but I think I might have approached things differently. I looked at the wild bugger one more time and got out of there. I needed to find a place to sleep.

I soon came across the Town's Inn, which looked like an ideal place to solve my daily sleeping dilemma.

The inn consisted of two buildings, both of which were constructed in the 1840s, which had me delighted with a familiar historical-place-loving buzz. I stayed in the building called The Mountain House. It had a few private rooms, as well as a hostel dorm-style room. I asked for a bed in the hostel, but was given a private room for the price of the hostel bed by the inn's kind owner.

After a satisfying night of sleep tucked into as many handmade quilts as I could pile onto myself, I took a stroll around town on streets frozen in another time. I was high on history. This stroll also involved stopping at a shop to eat a sandwich not of my own making, which was a bigger treat than you may realize. I also paid a visit to the Appalachian Trail Conservancy, the organization that manages the 2,100+ mile long Appalachian Trail. It's a daunting task, but they have always been up to the challenge. Growing up in Maine, the A.T. was my playground and the place where my wanderlust was first ignited. It only seemed right that I stop in at its official headquarters. I met a couple of battered looking section hikers there and talked to the staff for a while.

The conservancy building housed a giant topographical map of the entire Appalachian Trail. It was a shocking way to see the terrain that A.T. travelers have to deal with. I found Saddleback Mountain on the map, one of my favorite hikes in Maine. Right next to it I could see Rangeley, where I'd lived for the last year with Alana. It seemed like the universe was trying to send me reminders of her and home whenever it could. The night before, I hitched a ride to a local grocery store, and on the way there the man who picked me up said, "You're from Maine? No way! I used to live in Rangeley!"

Heading back over the river to the C&O that afternoon, I stopped for a few minutes to talk to a friendly hobo who was hanging out/living under the bridge. Then I continued down my gravel home, one step at a time.

~

A few days after Harpers Ferry, I found myself in the charming town of Williamsport, Maryland. The walk there had been peaceful, with views of farms with towering barns and fertile fields to my right and the slowly receding Potomac to my left. There were historical signs to read every so often, which I enjoyed. Most of them mentioned how Confederate Civil War General Robert E. Lee had battled with not only the Union Army, but also with the flooding Potomac River during his time in the area. It had prevented him from retreating to the relative safety of West Virginia on numerous occasions. I could picture General Lee standing on the river's soggy banks and cursing its bloated waters. Our journeys had that in common.

As I entered Williamsport I met some men who were fishing. They appeared to be rednecks of the highest order. There were four or five of them there and they were all dressed in full camouflage from head to toe. This would have been perfectly understandable for hunting purposes, but they were fishing. Each one of them had chewing tobacco packed tightly into their lower lips.

After exchanging hellos and explaining why I was walking around with Wilson on my back, the first thing one of the guys asked me was, "So, do ya jerk off in yer tent?" The question surprised me. It was a strange thing to ask someone you just met.

I nervously laughed and replied, "No."

"I'll tell ya what buddy, I'd be up in those woods rubbin' one out every night!" he shouted back while starting to laugh as the last word left his mouth. In unison, his tobacco chewing, camo-wearing backwoods buddies let out series of thunderous laughs as I stood there in awkward silence. They filed back over to the "crick" without saying another word. I didn't realize it at the time, but invasive questions such as that one would actually become a regular occurrence on the walk.

It was there in Williamsport on that fine sunny day that I unexpectedly learned I was a college graduate. I had attended a small community college back in Maine to play basketball, that's it. It was a good school, but actually learning things in a classroom was not something I cared about in the least. The basketball court received the majority of my focus. I was there for three years having a good time, playing some ball, and hanging out with friends. I quietly left school after my last semester, during which I actually dropped a class and stopped being a full time student.

As I sat on a bench in downtown Williamsport, my phone rang with a call from a Maine area code. It was someone calling from the college I had so haphazardly attended a couple years earlier. I was surprised when they informed me that I somehow had enough credits to earn an associates degree. I had simply never bothered to check if I could graduate when I left. I wanted to travel. You don't need a degree for that.

The lady on the phone said she would send me a fancy piece of paper saying that I had an associates degree in general studies, all I had to do was come in and sign a couple of documents. I told her I was traveling and wouldn't be home to sign anything for at least six months. She asked where I was traveling, so I told her, which ended up being a good thing, because she said that we could skip the whole document signing process. My degree would be sent by mail to my mom's house right away.

To celebrate my newly acquired real-world credentials, I splurged on a hotel room in Williamsport. I figured that a shower was a good idea, mostly because I had some visitors coming to hang out with me that night. These visitors would be fellow cross-country walkers, Mitchell and Christine, a married couple who had completed their own trek several years earlier. They would probably tolerate my hiker smell because they had once been smelly hikers themselves, but I convinced myself that I deserved a shower and a bed to sleep in. After all, I'd just graduated from college. That's sort of a big deal.

Mitchell and Christine turned out to be the best sort of company. They bought me food and ice cream, took me bowling, and did their best to convince me that what I was doing wasn't as crazy as it still seemed. They had a precious little daughter, Piper, who joined us for the evening. While hanging out with them, it was the first time of my life up to that point when I thought that having a child looked at least somewhat enjoyable. Mitchell and Christine were having fun, smiling, and didn't look miserable at all about being parents to the little bundle of cuteness that was Piper. In fact, they looked pretty damn pleased about the whole thing. This realization surprised me. The thought of children and responsibility had always scared me beyond words. A college degree in the morning and a few halfway serious thoughts about becoming an actual person someday — I felt like I was maybe growing up a little bit.

Chapter 5: Getting Lost

Several days after leaving Williamsport, I set foot in Pennsylvania for what I thought would be at least a couple of weeks. My visit to The Keystone State was, in reality, much more short lived.

My first morning there began like any other. I hit the road knowing I had an important right turn a couple of miles ahead, and watched for it diligently while taking in the cool morning air and views of farms nestled between rolling hills. One concept I was not familiar with at the time, however, was that roads often changed names from county to county when you got out in the middle of nowhere in Pennsylvania. The road I was looking for technically did not exist. I had unknowingly passed my turn somewhere along the way.

I became lost to the point that I didn't know up from down, so I stopped to ask a lady for directions as she worked on her lawn. She appeared to be a woman in her twenties, but ended up being probably 14 or 15 years old. She looked frightened when I greeted her and ran inside her house to call for her dad. Like things weren't already awkward enough, the man who came out of the house was frightening in the most vivid sense of the word.

The guy was at least 6' 4" tall and was wearing a cutoff black shirt that displayed muscular arms that were bigger around than my head. His entire bald head was covered by a spider web tattoo. The whole thing. It extended from the back of his neck all the way up and over the top of his head and down his forehead to his eyebrows. He looked like someone who would have been a World Wrestling Federation wrestler in the mid-'90s. Either that or a serial killer. I could practically hear a chainsaw starting and pictured myself running through the woods from the spider-web-headed killer, only to trip over a log, leaving myself ready for dismembering and a shallow grave.

Just as I was about to shout, "PLEASE DON'T KILL ME!" he walked up and said, "Hey man, how can I help you?" in a giant but friendly voice.

"Ah, um, eh, I'm ah, lost, and um, was wondering if you could, ah, help me figure out where I am," I mumbled with sweat pouring down my face from underneath my winter hat. He laughed, then told me where I was, where I had gone wrong, and what I needed to do to correct myself.

Problems arose again quickly after I left his yard. I realized that the sheer terror brought on by being in the spider-headed-tattoo-man's presence had distracted me from actually listening to the directions he had given me. Stomping angrily and swearing loudly, I meandered deeper into the Pennsylvania countryside in the complete wrong direction.

After another hour of this nonsense, I decided to try another attempt at directions. I saw a friendly looking home with two cars in the driveway, and decided that it would be a suitable place to ask. Walking up slowly and hoping that the person who answered the door wouldn't have a head-covering tattoo of any kind, I rang the doorbell.

A sweet old man answered the door, and I told him about my predicament. He said the closest store of any kind where I might be able to get a phone signal or map was about four miles away. I took a deep breath and actually listened to his directions.

About an hour and a half later, I rounded a corner to see The Road Kill Cafe. My dream of finding a place to charge my dead phone and possibly even get a detailed local map was coming true. The building's blue Amoco sign and outdoor Coke machine were encouraging sights. Or so I thought. After checking inside, I found that the place actually had no cell phone service or Wi-Fi and not one single map for sale. They did, however, have a damn good burger, which I enjoyed with a bottle of Coke. I had no idea what I was going to do when my meal was finished, but it was a welcomed break from worrying.

I sat down and took in my surroundings. Any establishment with the phrase "Road Kill" in its name usually has some character to it. It was the first of many all-in-one type stores I would experience on the walk. You could get groceries, liquor, gas, a sit-down meal, a new jacket or boots, ammunition, and almost any other necessity of the Appalachian hill dweller, all under one roof. Maps seemed to be the only thing they did not actually have.

The couple at the table next to me asked what I was up to as I ate, so I explained my miserable day to them. They made several looks at one another that if vocalized would be something like, *Should we help the poor bugger?* After the silent deliberation, they offered me a ride back to Maryland and the C&O, where I could walk peacefully on trails to Cumberland and then reevaluate my route from there. I figured that their offer was a sign and took them up on it without hesitation. It meant some backtracking and probably a major route change down the line, but anything sounded better than wandering down into another nameless, black hole of a Pennsylvania valley.

I went to the front of the store to pay for my meal before heading out. The cashier said, "You're all set honey, somebody covered that for ya." Surprised, I asked who it was so I could thank them. She said,

"They're already gone, but I'll tell them for ya next time they come in." I thanked her and made my way out to the parking lot feeling full and happy.

My rescuers and I rode up curvy hill roads and down into deep valleys on the way to the C&O. They loaded me up with six bottles of water when we made a pit stop at their house, then we continued toward the canal in their blue Ford pickup truck. The man was tall with white hair and a gray beard. His wife was stocky and was wearing a letterman jacket like a high school kid would wear. I thought about how maybe her husband was a football star once upon a time and that he had let her wear his jacket when they were high school sweethearts. Perhaps she just never bothered to get a different one.

After a while we arrived at the towpath, my old and familiar friend. Crows flew overhead and welcomed me back. The countless blue herons that called the area home were happy to have someone to fly along with again as I walked on the trail. Turtles leapt off of logs as I approached with dazzling style, their splashes letting me know I was back in nature and on a path that at that point seemed familiar and comfortable.

Up ahead I walked through the 3,118 foot Paw Paw Tunnel. The Paw Paw was an expanse of darkness that people had been warning me about for several days. This wasn't necessarily because it was dangerous, but because its deep darkness could be nerve-racking to cross through, depending on the time of day that a person made an attempt. The ultimate challenge was making your way through it without the help of a light. Against my better judgment, I opted for the challenge.

The walking path through the tunnel was a wooden walkway with a sturdy brick wall to its left and a flimsy wooden guardrail to its right. Murky canal water sat ten feet or so underneath the walkway. Into the Appalachian hill I went, tripping over my own feet and singing to try to lighten the mood and shake the feeling that my impending doom was just ahead in the shadows. The darkness was intimidating. The fact that it was an overcast day outside made it even darker than it usually would be in there. Virtually no light was coming in from either of the tunnel's openings. I began getting claustrophobic and every noise around me was startling. After what seemed like an entire day, I finally escaped the tunnel with my nerves completely shot and praised the sky that I had finally reached the pinhole of light I'd been nervously stumbling toward for nearly three-quarters of a mile.

Aside from being a black, damp tunnel of terror, the Paw Paw Tunnel is actually a significant engineering achievement. The many millions of hand-placed bricks that encase the hand-dug tunnel are a true marvel of human grit.

Behind its impressive appearance, however, is a history of utter financial failure and hardship. The tunnel was completed at over 500% of its original projected cost and took twelve years to build (1836-1848) instead of the estimated two the construction company claimed it would. Workers went unpaid, fights broke out between groups of immigrant workers. Some murders were even rumored to have taken place there during the construction. But hey, totally worth it so a few brave souls each day can face their fear of the dark, right?

~

About ten miles outside of Cumberland, which marks the end of the C&O Canal, I stopped at a unique looking store. Feeling chipper because of the clear skies above and the knowledge that there were only a few more hours of walking until I could gorge myself on bad food and sleep in a motel bed, I approached the door and it opened with the faint chime of a bell.

    The place was constructed of cinder blocks and covered partly by cracking wooden shingles, all coated with peeling white paint. The gas pumps that once stood in front of the store had long since been removed. All that remained outside were a couple of soda machines and a worn out ice chest. A neon OPEN sign flickered in the window. The dozens of flyers and advertisements that had been placed around it over the years made it difficult to see inside. An antique sign hung from a black metal post that read "Hershey's Ice Cream" followed by "Harry M. Shryock Groceries" in red, white, and baby blue lettering. There appeared to be a tiny apartment attached to the store. I imagined its humble owners calling it home, graciously unlocking a squeaky front door to a past-closing-time knock from a neighbor in need of something that couldn't wait until morning.

    I would only expect an eccentric character as the proprietor of such an establishment, and the little lady that greeted me when I walked in the door certainly didn't disappoint. She was about five feet tall, probably less, with short white hair and a wrinkled face. She didn't wear glasses, though she clearly needed them. Both of her eyes gazed blankly in different directions. I could tell she didn't quite know where I was, and only knew of my presence because of the bell that had rung on the door, or maybe by spotting my dark figure weaving through the ancient shelves and displays. The cash register she stood behind must have been state-of-the-art- when it hit the market 40 or 50 years back. She could probably recall the day it rang up its first total.

This was a textbook example of a mom-and-pop store. This delightful lady was mom.

Canned food of an unknown age sat in dusty lines on the wooden shelves. There were a couple of drink coolers that showed dings and a bit of rust from years of service. Bent metal racks had bags of chips and a sparse assortment of candy bars to choose from. Everything was worn out. I couldn't ignore the sensation that I was doing something resembling time travel. After taking a few laps around the tiny store I grabbed two MoonPies and a bottle of Coke, glass bottle of course.

I approached the check-out counter and asked the little lady if she took credit cards. She replied, "Nope, only cash hun." Her whole face moved as she talked and her buggy eyes blinked with each syllable she spoke.

"That's fine, I've got some," I said, then waited for her to begin totaling up my three items. Now, this was a process. I'd say that it took her at least a few minutes to add the prices together. She began by grabbing a wide magnifying glass, apparently preferring that option to glasses as a way of improving her questionable vision. She then painstakingly started investigating each item to find the price sticker on it. Once she accomplished this, she would move ever so slowly over to the manual cash register while still using the magnifying glass to see, and aggressively punch in each of the digits for the price. The process would then be repeated for the next item. Finally, she gave me a total that surprised me a bit. It was something like $1.75.

"That seems low, are you sure?"

"Ayup, it's right," she said back with a smile.

I paid the whopping amount she required of me and cracked open my bottle of Coke with an opener that was bolted to the counter. "Be careful out there!" she screeched as I opened the door and walked outside, the door bell ringing behind me.

~

    Cumberland sat just ahead, and it became clear that I had underestimated its size. Thrown back into a world of speed and exhaust fumes, the serene wooded path I had grown so fond of became a distant memory.
    Clouds came rolling in from the surrounding hills as I found my way to where the C&O ended. I went to a nearby Dominos to get a large pizza before finding a hotel. When the cashier learned what I was doing, she threw in a two-liter soda and a large order of boneless buffalo wings for free. I decided I would attempt to eat it all.
    Unfortunately, due to the high degree of disorientation I experience whenever I enter a town that has more than two or three streets, I still had over a mile to walk to get to the closest hotel. I limped down the road, over a busy bridge, and down into the bowels of Cumberland while balancing my feast carefully across my chest and still lugging a 50+ pound Wilson.
    A young lady in a compact two-door car stopped at an intersection ahead of me and waved for me to come over. There was a baby in the backseat and a man who appeared to be her boyfriend or husband sat on the passenger side. I shuffled ahead to the intersection and she said, "Hey, you're hot! Need a ride?"
    The guy in the passenger seat gave her an angry look, then gave me an even angrier one, so I rushed out a "Thank you, I'm all set," and made my way around the car to the other side of the street. I looked like a homeless pizza delivery man, and a really bad one at that, so I'm not sure what she saw in me there.

The hotel finally came into view, and I walked into the lobby just as the rain started to pour down outside. The timing could not have been better. I got to my room, showered, and then ate the whole pizza, all of the buffalo wings, and drank nearly the entire two-liter soda, all while watching TV. It was many fat American stereotypes personified.

After a day off in Cumberland due to bad weather, with the highlight of the day being the purchase of a new umbrella, I found myself nearing West Virginia. U.S. Route 220 led me down to the fast approaching border of The Mountain State. In McCoole, Maryland, I stopped at a gas station for a snack. Several people there warned me of the below-freezing temperatures and snow that had been forecasted for the upcoming night.

Sure enough, as I walked down the last hill of Maryland and over a bridge into Keyser, West Virginia, snowflakes started to fall. A *Welcome to West Virginia* flurry set the tone for the cold nights and difficult miles ahead.

Chapter 6: Into The Appalachians

The excitement of my second state line crossing (I'm not counting Pennsylvania) was cut short, as the situation became one of survival due to a barrage of snowflakes and temperatures dipping down into the 20s. Not wanting to spend the money required for a hotel room despite the blistering cold, I decided to hike to the west side of Keyser. I thought that there I might be able to find a sheltered and secluded place in the woods before the mercury dropped much further.

I hadn't even made it halfway through town before a lady in a maroon car pulled into a roadside parking lot and waved me over to her rolled down window. Her name was Deanna. She wanted to know if I had a place to sleep for the night. She looked to be in her forties, had her hair in a neat ponytail, and wore glasses. After telling her that I didn't know where I'd be staying, she said, "My husband is a contractor. He's working on a church just up the road. Hop in and I'll take you there. I'm sure you can camp on the property." Elated about the prospective camping location, I jumped into her car for the short ride. Being a mom of two kids, Deanna asked about my mom and how she felt about me being out on the road all alone. I told her she was fine with it, but she didn't believe me.

We arrived at the church and I was introduced to Deanna's husband, Johnny. He was a quiet man, but had an intense energy about him. His employees, several of whom I met, respected him unquestionably. I got the feeling that he was a fair and supportive boss if you did the work right, but if you slacked off for a minute he would rip you a new one.

I explained what I was doing and my need for a place to camp. He replied "Well, how about we just put you up in a hotel for the night?" Feeling slightly embarrassed, I said that the offer was kind, but that he didn't need to do such a thing. I still wasn't accustomed to accepting the help of complete strangers, especially when that help would cost them money.

"I'd like to. Let me make a couple phone calls," he said.

Johnny ended up arranging a room for me at the Keyser Inn, which was back in town near where Deanna had stopped for me earlier. He drove me there, paid for the room, and I found myself lying on a bed about to take a hot shower with the widest smile possible on my face. Deanna would be back in 30 minutes to pick me up and take me out for dinner. We ended up going to a nearby Mexican restaurant and must have talked for at least two hours non-stop. Just before going to sleep, I stared out the motel room window and watched the light snow fall for a while.

~

I had my eyes set on Mount Storm, a tiny town with an intimidating name.

With miles of curvy switchbacks between Keyser and my goal, some with 8-9 percent grades, I knew it would be a tough day physically. With that being said, I felt energized by finally being able to tread on Highway 50, one of America's original cross-country driving routes. Instead of just crossing it on the way to somewhere else like I had already done a few times, good ol' 50 would be my home for much of the remainder of the walk. As I got onto 50, I thought about the fact that the same road I was standing on in rural West Virginia ended in Sacramento, California, just a short distance from San Francisco. Although thousands of miles sat between where I was and the other coast, I found the idea strangely comforting.

Heading out of Keyser on the trek to Mount Storm, a lady stopped and gave me a $20 bill. I made my way toward the wilderness $20 richer and with all systems running smoothly on mountain air. A bubbling roadside creek sounded like sweet music. Following it, I was guided into the Appalachian foothills.

The walking proved to be as difficult as I had assumed it would be, and then some. With awful physical struggles usually come great rewards, especially while moving upward, and this stretch was no exception. Escaping from the flatlands reminded me of home. The endless vista of mountains covered in bare trees with dead orange and brown leaves littering the landscape looked strikingly similar to western Maine. I could have been walking in my own hometown. The road's narrow shoulders, which were cracked and crumbling, acted as final safe havens for those making even the slightest of driving errors. Without them, all that would be left after such a mistake would be a precarious drop into the valley below. The white and yellow road lines were faded and even nonexistent in certain places. To think that the same neglected road I was standing on was a six lane mega-highway only a couple hundred miles to the east was almost unimaginable.

From above, the view would have looked like a series of "S" shaped paths carved into the side of the mountains. I walked one mile to make 1/4 of a mile of progress up the unrelenting hills, but thrived in the difficulty of the walking. Sweating and yelling, I challenged for more out of boredom, frustration, or possibly even the twisted desire to punish myself for being idiotic enough to actually do such a thing.

Farms perched on little knolls, or sometimes right on the side of the steepness, provided a glimpse into farm life in the high mountains. Cows mooed and sheep bleated, their calls echoing through the placid forest. It was cold. My breath hung suspended in the air. Water trickled out of culverts and splashed onto the piles of jagged ice sitting below them. Winter was still in effect up there, much different from the 70-degree weather I had experienced just a few days earlier in Maryland.

I passed a garage of some sort, a cinder block building with a green metal sliding door. Its windows were boarded up and the structure featured several colors of paint. It looked like your average West Virginia multi-purpose building, but attached to the front of it was a massive green Interstate highway sign that read: ORLANDO DISNEY WORLD - LEFT LANE. Seeing this caused my oxygen deprived brain to freeze up in confusion for a second before I realized I was in fact not anywhere near Disney World. I thought about how much I wished the sign were right.

Exhausted from the day's chilly 20 mile trudge, I came up over one last hill and found myself in Mount Storm. It wasn't the kind of place you wanted to be with plummeting temperatures and a snow filled overnight forecast.

Walking into the local gas station/hardware store/restaurant/meeting place, I grabbed a drink to sip on as I tried to warm up, then began looking for tips on a place where I might be able to camp. The young woman behind the store's counter was not so pleasant at first, but once we had talked for a few minutes, she changed for the better. This seemed to be the way with people in West Virginia. Mean looks at first, but it was really all a front. Inside, I found them to be welcoming, enthusiastic, and caring folks, for the most part.

I learned that a park just up the road was available for camping. It even had a covered picnic area with a wall to keep me out of the wind. I left the store and began the show that was getting the monstrosity known as Wilson lifted and strapped onto my knotted and sore shoulders and back. As I was doing this, a loud, four-door truck rumbled off Highway 50 and into the store's parking area. A man who was unmistakably West Virginian hopped out of it. He was wearing well-used jeans, work boots, and the permanent *I've worked my ass off all day and just want a beer* scowl that most manual laborers tend to have after a long day.

The man asked what I was doing as he watched me struggle to wrangle Wilson into submission. After telling him, he said that about a half a mile back down Highway 50 there was a house he was renovating, and that I was welcome to stay in it. Tim was his name. He was a rougher looking character and seemed like he had lived through his share of long nights. I immediately liked him. "There's no water, but there's a space heater and a few power cords up there. Not fancy, but it will keep you out of the wind," he said.

I leapt into his warm truck, and he drove me to the house. After thanking him several times, he said, "No problem. I used to be homeless once, went to prison too. I know what it's like to not have a place to stay. I was in real bad shape, I'll tell ya. But got out and got my life together. Started my own salvage company and now I'm rich."

I told him how things had fallen apart for me back home and that the trip was saving me. It was a deep talk for people who had known each other for approximately five minutes total.

The place was under construction, as Tim had said. Sawhorses, tools, and lumber laid out everywhere. A hearty layer of white, powdery drywall dust covered the floor and got into every nook and cranny of the building. Within minutes I was covered in it and looked like a powdered sugar doughnut.

I laid my sleeping bag out on the plywood floor and was soon inside it battling the constant shivering that ended up lasting throughout the night. The temperature dropped to fifteen degrees. Not much sleep was had. I was cold, despite having all my clothes on, which included two jackets, gloves, a hat, plus an extra fleece blanket that Deanna and Johnny had given me back in Keyser.

A space heater taunted me from the corner of the room. I just couldn't bring myself to use it. As Tim dropped me off he said, "The only rule is this — don't burn the house down." I didn't feel like taking any chances, as I typically don't play very well with any sort of machinery, and that was one rule I was determined not to break.

~

The following afternoon, the sleepy town of Aurora appeared ahead after a pleasant walk through a pine forest. I searched around town for a camping lead. Nothing presented itself, so I went with my go-to backup plan of finding a place outside of town in the woods. The sun was going down rapidly, which meant a significant temperature drop was on the way.

Just a few houses from the end of town, where the silent wilderness began once again, I heard a raspy shout from my left.

"YOU WANT SOME COOKIEEEES?"

I turned toward the voice, but could not see anyone. There was a house with a deck guarded by a row of fir trees nearby. I figured it could have been the source of the call. Being of cold mind and feeling desperate for something other than Pop Tarts and PB&J, I shouted back to whomever was behind the trees, "Hell yeah I want some cookies!"

The mystery cookie person made their way around the trees. He was fairly tall, definitely over six feet, almost bald, and sporting a thin, whitish-gray beard. Willard was his name. We stood in his kitchen and talked as I packed away peanut butter no-bake cookies as fast as I could. We chatted about all things walking across America and he said, "Where you camping tonight?"

"I don't know. Was heading out of town to find a place in the woods."

"Not anymore you're not. I've got a guest room here for you. It's supposed to get into the teens tonight, too cold for camping. I'll make you a nice big dinner," he said.

Sold. With the choice to either hang out around the house for a bit or accompany Willard to his father's farm to deliver a few bales of hay, I chose to join in on the delivery. It was the farm he had grown up on. I could tell he wanted to me to see it.

We clattered off Highway 50 and down seemingly endless dirt roads in Willard's beat up boat of a car. Further and further back into the wilds of West Virginia hill country we bounced, kicking up dust and dodging potholes. After a while we emerged into the valley that contained his father's farm, which was surrounded by hilly pasture land and scattered clumps of trees.

Willard's father's house was small and looked cozy. A timeworn barn constructed of not-so-tightly spaced vertical boards sat next to it. The barn had a heavily rusted metal roof. Entire sections of its rusted sheeting were missing or bent to one side or the other. The constant wind that day in the valley got under the sections of the gnarled metal and slammed them back down at a consistent rhythm. Several other sheds and garages were spread around, housing various pieces of machinery and the many other tools necessary for survival in the lonely hills.

We approached the house and entered it through a creaky front door. A tall, wiry man with broad, well-worked hands sat at a table in the kitchen under a dim lamp. He was bald, had a Santa Claus type beard, and was wearing faded jean overalls. Leaning back in his chair, he stuffed his face with some sort of small, white, carrot-like vegetable. He nibbled off small sections of them bit by bit with his front teeth until they were gone. A couple of tables were stacked with canned everything in the kitchen, the bounty of the previous spring's crop. A little Chihuahua nipped at my ankles.

I nervously introduced myself. The first thing he quietly said to me was, "Ya want a ramp?"

Feeling foolish for having no clue what he was talking about, I said, "Umm... I don't know what you mean."

"A ramp, here, take one," he said as his outstretched hand revealed one of the white carrot things he was chomping on.

"I'm warning you, these things will stay on your breath for about three days. They're a really strong sort of onion that grow naturally in the hills here," Willard rasped at me as he chuckled to himself.

Never having eaten a ramp before, I took it, stared at it for a few seconds, and then looked up at Willard and his father. They were both gazing at me wide-eyed and expectant like I was holding a stick of dynamite. Willard's father had a playful smirk on his face. I tossed it into my mouth and chewed, if for no other reason than to please the old mountain man. Willard wasn't kidding about the potent flavor of the little root. It was actually quite tasty, but I imagine it would have been much better cooked with something. And yes, I was reminded of its flavor for a long time after. Brushing my teeth proved to be of no use.

We unloaded a couple bales of hay, said hello to Ben and Jerry — the two young cows on the farm — and made our way out of the valley and back to the solitary vein of civilization through the mountains, Highway 50. "I love that house. Grew up there as a kid. We used to have to walk several miles just to get to the school bus stop. The water in the house was fed down from a spring in the hills through a pipe, still comes in that way today. We didn't even have indoor plumbing until I was 12 or 13," Willard said as we drove off. Pride for the place beamed from his face as he spoke. Life in the hills is simple and hard at the same time, and I quickly learned that the people who call them home do so very intentionally. They wouldn't have things any other way. I thought of my own home and how disconnected I felt from it, wondering why that was the case.

Back at the house, Willard prepared a dinner large enough for a football team. He told me about his passion for cooking and that he had done some catering work in the past, but had never pursued it further. He rarely cooked anymore, as it was just him around the house. Despite this, Willard's skills in the kitchen had not gotten rusty. Steaks, potatoes, salad, biscuits, green beans, homemade apple butter, steamed vegetables, and cookies were passed my way as he labored over the hot stove. He was in his element. The food coma that came as a result of this epic feast had me ready for bed soon after we finished eating. I passed out early in the guest room.

In the morning, I found out it had snowed during the night. Slush and ice covered the road. With an offer from Willard to take the day off at the house, but feeling the push to get out of the mountains and back to flatter ground, I stepped down Willard's front steps and out into the wintry wonderland. Wilson was reluctant to cooperate and felt heavy, probably because he was loaded down with a bulging bag of pepperoni rolls that Willard had made for me.

The first breath I took after leaving Willard's was the freshest I can recall ever breathing. The saturated mountaintop air expanded my lungs to their full capacities. Every vein in my head jumped for joy. It actually made me dizzy for a moment.

The road was slippery. My boots were wet from the slush almost immediately, but the rising morning sun brought a warmth to my face that I knew would melt away the night's snowfall soon enough. I thought of the last time I had fled down a snowy highway. It was back in Maine when I left everything I loved behind. I was a month into the walk, but still had no clue why I was doing what I was doing. My stomach turned almost every second of the day from the fear that I had messed up the only good thing that would ever happen to me. Alana was on my mind as I trudged through the snow.

There were certainly happy moments that I was finding in the beautiful landscapes and kind people along my path, but my mind always reverted back to the things that still hurt me so badly. I couldn't seem to escape them. What distance was theoretically supposed to help with, it seemed to be making worse.

With my walking stick, I took frustrated swings at icicles that hung from the exposed rock faces just a few feet from the road, my ever changing and still foreign home. There was a thin coat of white as far as I could see across the rising hills and dipping valleys. Finally, I began my descent toward lower elevations. Water from the snowmelt rushed along the sides of the road and sometimes straight down it. It was nice to see proof that the days were getting warmer.

Chapter 7: Succeed Or Die

A lot of the homes I walked by in the coming miles were more like shacks than actual houses. Many looked barely livable but had brand new pickup trucks and two or three four-wheelers in their driveways. I saw the occasional Confederate flag waving. Every house had satellite TV, regardless of how dilapidated it was. As one man I met told me, "The official state flower of West Virginia is the satellite dish."

Spurred on by the excitement of seeing new things and the lack of anything better to do except continue onward, I had been pushing myself too hard in the cold weather. Sheer physical exhaustion was bound to catch up and punish me, and it did. There was certainly a lot of mental exhaustion going on as well. I missed being home. I missed knowing where I was going to sleep at night. Regrets piled into my thoughts.

So on March 27, my body just gave out. I fell to the ground and sat on the side of the road, crying. Quitting the walk became an actual thought. I thought about a lot of things on that frozen ground. Why had I always ended up letting people down? Why did most people not seem to take me seriously about the walk? Why did I end up all alone back in Maine with a bottle in my hand and feeling sorry for myself?

It was gradually becoming more and more clear to me that I was an unreliable person. My word was no good to anyone. I had chosen to navigate my existence by following the path of least resistance. When things got hard, I bailed. It was easier to run than to commit to something and pursue it in the face of danger and under the possibility of failure.

The time had come for me to chase a dream against all odds. Succeed or die. A stagnant and uninspired lifestyle had nothing left to teach me. This was how the walk suddenly became a mission for truth. I absolutely had to learn what it really meant to be alive and do something that mattered. The voyage could no longer be bogged down in expectations, regrets, and escape plans. Fuck the past, everyone else's opinions, and even my own opinions. Just walk, breathe, see, feel, and not even try to make sense of it all. It was time to simply let things be what they were.

It would certainly be a struggle. I wouldn't come close to achieving a state of relative peace for a couple of months, but I felt optimistic knowing that I was at least on the right path. As I got my feet back under me on the side of that road and tightened up Wilson's shoulder straps with my numb fingers, I decided that I was really going to walk across the country, even if it would kill me. It almost would on many occasions.

~

Cool Springs Park, a treasure of Highway 50 and days gone by, was the first true oasis of the walk. It was a place so well located along my map of roads and circumstances that I questioned whether or not some divine power had placed it there just for me. I arrived there just a mile after breaking down on the side of the road and thinking about quitting.

Cool Springs Park stands as one of the few most recognizable remnants of the pre-Interstate highway days in West Virginia. As I mentioned in passing before, Route 50 was once one of the more popular, and only, cross-country driving routes in America. Places like Cool Springs Park, and various other establishments and towns scattered throughout the mountains of West Virginia, flourished because of this. But the peak years for these outposts eventually began to phase out as more drivers opted for newly constructed multi-lane highways with more direct routes and higher speed limits, causing many of them to slowly fall into obscurity. I saw the skeletons of these places that had been left behind in many regions across the country. Cool Springs Park, for whatever reason, remained through it all and appeared to be thriving. Part restaurant, hardware store, souvenir shop, grocery store, clothing store, and gas station, it had everything a traveler needed.

Even with the ability to buy a t-shirt displaying my love of West Virginia, a new pair of boots, a sledge hammer, or a gallon of milk, I opted for the tremendous food options Cool Springs Park had to offer instead. The house specialty seemed to be the foot-long hotdog. I put away two of them in just a few minutes while sitting in one of the swiveling orange chairs at the diner counter.

I watched silently as people filtered in and out of the restaurant. Locals chatted with one another as they nursed cups of coffee at the counter, in no particular hurry to do anything. The brave tourists who chose Highway 50 over the Interstate milled through racks of cheesy trinkets and bought postcards and t-shirts. It was refreshing to be in society and feel at least fairly normal, aside from a damp Wilson leaning up against my seat.

As he was heading out the door, I saw a man do a double take when he noticed my soggy partner in crime, and he changed directions to come talk to me. We chatted for a few minutes and he invited me to stop by his tree nursery the next day, which was somewhere just up the road.

After paying my waitress for my meal, I asked if there was any chance that I could camp next to the building for the night. She referred me to her manager, who gave me a quick yes. A few minutes later, my tent was set up and I was dozing off in the late afternoon sun.

~

After another grueling uphill section of switchbacks west of Cool Springs Park that had me so turned around I didn't know east from west, I once again commenced the knee-jarring act of walking out of the mountains down a nine percent grade. The steepness continued for well over four miles. My toes begged for mercy as they jammed into the fronts of my boots with each step.

After reaching flatter ground, I rounded a corner and found the tree nursery where I was supposed to stop in for a visit. I found the man who had told me to come by at Cool Springs Park the previous day. He looked surprised that I had shown up. Lynn was his name. Lynn stood at about 6' 2" and had gray hair. He wore a dusty flannel shirt and jeans with work boots. We talked for a minute as I watched him struggle with some blueberry bushes that he was trying to dig up and ship halfway across the country to a customer. It looked like difficult work, so I offered him a hand, but he said he wanted to take a break anyway. He reached into his truck, pulled out a couple of beers, and we took a seat on the hillside. I liked what "taking a break" meant in West Virginia.

Lynn dove right into telling me his life story. I was particularly intrigued as he told me about his family's military background. His grandfather had served in World War I and experienced brutal combat. After being seriously wounded during a firefight, he laid dying on the ground as German soldiers waded through the dead and injured, finishing those who were still alive off with their signature Luger handguns. His grandfather was approached by one of these men and shot at point blank range in the head. The bullet, by some sort of miracle, passed through his skull in just the right way that he was able to survive the wound. He was later found by friendly forces and nursed back to health.

Lynn's father had bravely served in World War II and saw heavy action in the Pacific theater. These notorious missions into the Pacific islands turned the war, but the resulting losses were staggering. After seeing horrendous combat, some of the fiercest in our nation's military history, he returned home. Tragically, only about a week after getting back, he was killed in a car accident. It was the kind of thing you hear about from time to time, but can't believe that it really happens.

Lynn was drafted to go to Vietnam right out of high school. He soon found himself a third generation soldier in the U.S. military, bravely representing the same ideals that his grandfather and father had. He was sent overseas as a long range artillery specialist. He shared stories of combat, the strategy behind long range artillery, and tales of the cobras that slithered into his barracks during the night. He was a storyteller, and a damn good one at that. I was captivated.

Lynn showed me around his impressive farm. There was a little bit of everything there including goats, cows, gardens, chickens, old farm dogs, and an assortment of other furry or feathery creatures. The place sprang with life in the still slightly dreary tail-end of winter. Wooden fences stretched far into the distance, their posts cut from crooked tree limbs.

In the afternoon we took a trip down the road to meet Lynn's brother, Stan. Lynn prepared me for the visit by saying, "Now, my brother Stan, he owns a handmade wooden utensils business, I'm taking you there to see how it works. Just a few years ago, Stan and his wife were living below the poverty line and barely making it on almost no money at all. Really struggling. Well, they would carve wooden spoons and forks for people as gifts because they couldn't afford to buy anything. One day, someone told them they should take their work to a craft fair, so they did. Get this, they made about as much as they had made during the whole year in that one day!"

Once this happened, Stan and Sue quickly realized they were onto something, and they went all in. Allegheny Treenware, their home-grown business, sits in an unassuming building just off Highway 50 in quiet Thornton, West Virginia. The quality of their work was noticed immediately after they began distributing their products, and Allegheny Treenware took off. Initially they were successful at craft fairs and shows in West Virginia, but as news of their talent began to spread, they found themselves in nation and world-wide markets. Their products appeared in *Southern Living* and *Martha Stewart Living*. The White House requested that they make an ornament for the First Family's Christmas tree, and they were invited to visit for a tour.

After a short drive, Lynn and I arrived at Allegheny Treenware. I met Stan and Sue outside, then followed them into the building that housed their various machines, wood supply, and employees. The first thing I noticed was that everyone seemed to be thrilled to be there. Working for a person like Stan, why wouldn't they be? I had never met a person who looked more pleased to be alive than Stan. He had a round white beard and his face flushed red when he laughed, glowing almost as brightly as his heavy-duty hunter orange Carhartt jacket. Stan in one word: jolly.

Stan led a tour through the facility. Spoons, forks, spatulas, whisks, ladles, bowls, cutting boards, and just about any other kitchen related item you could think up were in the works as we strolled around. Work stations were placed in an assembly line sort of formation. Employees at each station were responsible for one of the many steps that went into making handmade wooden products of the finest sort.

At one end of the building, the process began with a solid block of wood. By the time it reached the other end it was a smooth, finely crafted piece fit for use in even the most luxurious of homes and establishments. The finished pieces were organized into bins by what they were (spoons, forks, spatulas, etc.) then sent to the small group of ladies who spent their days chatting and woodburning the Allegheny Treenware logo and the type of wood that had been used to make the pieces into their handles. Stan picked out a spoon and fork for me as a gift. The spoon was made of Osage Orange, the fork of Dogwood.

While talking with the woodburning ladies in the back room of the building, Stan opened the refrigerator in the corner of the room and took out a large, clear bottle. I was about to have my first experience with eye watering, throat burning West Virginia moonshine. Stan and Lynn quickly took care of a couple shots, so I thought, *Hey, it can't be that bad.*

Stan poured about a quarter-inch worth of the clear liquid into the bottom of a cup and warned me to just take a small sip first. He and Lynn seemed adamant about a cautious approach to their homemade concoction. I put the cup to my lips and followed their suggestion. It was like drinking rubbing alcohol. The smell was what really got to me. It felt like it singed my nose hairs. With a twisted expression on my face, I downed the remaining 'shine and winced as the rocket fuel made its way to my stomach. I could feel the warmth of it all the way down, like a slowly spreading fire was rolling into my internal organs.

As this was happening, the Jennings brothers were grinning ear to ear. The woodburning ladies were rocking back and forth in their chairs laughing. I was a wholesome New England kid lost in the wilds of West Virginia, drinking moonshine, getting a real taste of mountain life. They were loving every second of it. Truth be told, so was I.

~

We were soon back at Lynn's farm, and he began preparing a meal of staggering proportions. He rustled up steaks the size of entire plates and almost two inches thick, freakishly large potatoes, fluffy biscuits, and a garden salad with homemade dressing. Milk from the cows and goats I had just met, along with cheese that was still in the aging process made from that same milk, sat in the refrigerator. Smoke and steam rose from the stove as we talked over the loud sizzling of steaks cooking.

The most amazing thing about the meal was that almost everything we ate was raised or grown within a hundred yards of the house we were eating it in. I stuffed myself until I was hardly able to move away from the table. I wasn't in a rush anyway, as Lynn was sharing story after story, and I could have listened endlessly.

Once the stories did slow down a bit, Lynn said, "You want to take a shower? I'll head out to the shed and get the fire going. Shouldn't be too long." Just like at Willard's father's house, the hot water in Lynn's home was heated by wood fire in a nearby shed, and then pumped into the house. Excited for my first wood fire heated shower, I patiently waited for the water to reach the right temperature.

Eventually it did. Or so I thought. Lynn said that I would be all set to go, so I made my way into the bathroom and turned on the water. I waited for a minute before giving it a test feel. Ice cold. Uh oh. I waited a few more minutes. Still cold. After deciding to suck it up because I would rather be frigid than rude, I hopped in. I'm sure that this ordeal would have been funny to watch. I bounced up and down and screamed profanities in my mind as I lathered some soap onto my body as quickly as possible. It turned out that cold showers on cold days were not much fun.

After a while of flopping around in the icy water, I was relatively clean. Feeling full and weary, I collapsed on Lynn's couch and slept like a rock until I got an early morning wakeup call from the farm's resident roosters.

~

Several days later, I got sick for the only time during the walk. I was staying with a couple, Paul and Sharon, when I began not feeling well. They lived on a vast West Virginia farm and were seasoned trail angels who had hosted several cross-country walkers over the years. In other words, I picked the right place to get sick. My head was throbbing, my appetite was zero, and I felt helplessly weak. I could barely walk up the stairs at their house. It wasn't good. I was scared that it could have been mono, which would have meant the walk was over.

I slept for nearly 16 straight hours at Paul and Sharon's. When I woke up, I felt like a million bucks.

Sharon made me some food, and I put it away quickly. Back to normal. One of those odd 24-hour bugs.

Leaving Paul and Sharon's, I hit the North Bend Rail Trail, a converted railroad track I would be following for over seventy miles. After a lot of road walking, I was ready for a quieter path. The trail would take me as far as Parkersburg, West Virginia. Ohio would be just a quick jump over the Ohio River away from there. I walked in light snow my first day on the trail.

Feeling full of energy from having such well-timed and gracious hosts, as well as from the oncoming promise of a new state line, I made my way into the small town of Petroleum on the North Bend.

~

The plan was to have a guy named Peter, who had volunteered to host me for a couple days, pick me up in Petroleum. I gave him a call as I got into town, if you could even call it that, and sat at a picnic table at a tiny park to wait for him to arrive.

Petroleum was a confusing place. The "town" was a small group of houses that sat in a sort of half-circle. Every house was visible to the others around it. I sat there in the middle of this area as people stared at me from their front porches and gave me mean looks.

A horse got loose from a pen at one of the houses and trotted on past me down the road. Its owners, wearing flannel shirts and sweatpants, pursued it while swearing loudly, huffing and puffing like they hadn't moved off the couch in weeks. With such fine entertainment as that, I wasn't in any hurry for Peter to arrive. After about half an hour he did, and we made our way to his house in his white Ford van.

My first thought as I entered his double-wide trailer was, *Wow, there are a lot of cats here*. Peter had seven cats. SEVEN CATS. I have never been overly allergic to the furry buggers, but at around the four or five cat mark my eyes begin to itch a bit. Luckily, Peter had a camper that he had bought especially for American Discovery Trail hikers that I could stay in next to his home. He was a diehard trail angel — a passionate, caring guy — the exact type of person a developing trail needs on its side.

We enjoyed some pizza for dinner and watched a History Channel documentary as we lounged around his mobile home. I hit the sack early, excited for easy walking ahead in the morning. I would be leaving Wilson's weightiness at Peter's for the day. I only had to cover the handful of miles between where I had left off in Petroleum and his home, where I'd spend the night one more time. Traveling lightly with a small day-pack sounded like a dream.

The morning walk quickly led me to another one of the small communities along the North Bend, where I had a destination already in mind. The previous day I had asked Peter if there was a place where I could grab a burger on my route, and he recommended a place right off the North Bend trail.

As I approached this establishment, I noticed that it was a significantly run down building. It wasn't quite what I was expecting from Peter's recommendation. Something in my gut told me that I shouldn't bother even walking through its door, but I decided to do it anyway. If for no other reason than to have a new mildly interesting experience in rural West Virginia.

I really should have listened to my gut. A muscular Rottweiler came charging at me with hell in his eyes as I got close to the door. I frantically swung my walking stick at it and yelled, "Get the hell back!" Thankfully, my defense tactic worked and I was able to gingerly tiptoe up to the door past the drooling beast.

The door had no windows of any kind on it. Upon trying to turn the handle, I realized that it was locked. The thing was, I knew that the place was open. Yet another red flag. As I stood there debating what to do for a few seconds, the door flung open in front of me and an exhausted looking man with dark bags under his eyes stuck his head out.

"I'm just looking for something to eat, are you open?"

"Uh, yeah, come on in. And ignore the dog, she won't hurt ya," he said.

I entered through the doorway and saw a bar, pool tables, a jukebox, and a couple of the shadiest looking characters. You know when you approach a group of people and get the feeling that they were just talking about you? It felt like that in there. A lingering awkwardness reminded me that I might not be such a welcomed guest. The place was dimly lit. Neon signs for cheap domestic beers glowed through the cloud of cigarette smoke that occupied every square inch of the bar.

After leaning Wilson up against one of the tables and taking a seat, one of the shady characters said, "Hey, whatcha doin' with that backpack?" to me.

I told him, and he said, "Well, damn! Let me get ya a beer! Budweiser good?"

"Ah, really appreciate that, but I'm ok," I said.

"What kind of beer do you want?" he said back sternly.

"Ok, Budweiser," I relented. I didn't want a beer at all, which admittedly is a rare occurrence for me, but accepting his offer seemed like a better alternative to offending him in any way. The man who offered me the beer was short, wearing jeans and a flannel shirt with a black baseball hat, and drinking straight whiskey. The sly smile he wore when he talked to me was absent of nearly all his teeth. He was profoundly intoxicated even though it was only around 11 AM. His friend was lanky at about 6' 6" and skinny. He had gray hair that extended down a bit further than his shoulders and was wearing thick-rimmed glasses. He was sipping a beer at the bar. He turned around from his seat to face me and slurred out, "Hiking, huh? I hitchhiked across the country, all the way to California and back when I was nine."

The food that I had ordered immediately after coming in the door, to be there for as little time as possible, came out surprisingly quickly. It was as I began to eat that things started to get weird. The two drunkards came up to my table to talk. Getting a closer view of them, I realized that they were tweakers. Meth heads. They were fidgeting around with a paranoid urgency. They stole rushed sips from their drinks and moved their glasses around from place to place. A meaningless conversation continued on and on. The shorter guy had meth mouth.

As I was about to finish my burger and fries, I noticed through the haze of smoke and neon that the two guys had gone to the corner of the room and were attempting to talk secretly to each other. They were nodding their heads my way, then turning their backs to talk so I couldn't hear or see what they were saying. Needless to say, it made me nervous. They were eyeing the progress that I was making on my meal closely and made their way past me to head outdoors right as I was finishing off the last of my fries. I paid in a hurry and hoped that they weren't waiting to rob or kill me outside.

I slowly opened the door and snuck by the Rottweiler. It looked at me with an uninterested gaze as it laid there, then closed its eyes and returned to its nap. The two guys were sitting in a small truck about twenty feet away. Of course, both of them got out as I came through the door.

The short one said, "Heeeey buddy, want to smoke some green?" and offered me a joint.

"Ah, no thanks man, I'm all set," I replied nervously. *Ok, everyone smokes weed, so nothing too bad so far*, I thought.

The big one said, "How ya doing on money?" *Well, here we go...*

I began to think that they were intending to rob me after all. I gripped my walking stick tightly and prepared to beat some tweakers. I swallowed hard and said, "Umm, I'm good. Don't carry much cash with me," hoping it would discourage them from wanting to see what I had to offer.

"Well, all I wanna say is, if you need some money, we've got a few ways around here that you can make it pretty quickly, if ya know what I mean," the short one stammered while raising his eyebrows in a way that he apparently deemed to be convincing, but instead came off as skin-crawlingly creepy.

I figured that I was either being solicited to perform some sort of act that is too disturbing for me to think about further, let alone write about, or being recruited to participate in the booming local drug trade. Nice.

I nervously replied "Ha, ha, thanks a lot, but I'm all set," and walked briskly to the road without saying another word. I jumped back down to the trail and high tailed it out of the area, all the while looking back with paranoid visions of that little truck rumbling down the path after me.

I couldn't wait to see Peter and thank him for his recommendation.

Chapter 8: Tall Tales And Old Hobo Spirits

I made the quick jaunt over the Ohio River into Belpre, Ohio after my second night at Peter's house. Ohio felt far from Delaware, mainly because it is, and I felt pleased about making it so far.

It was a serene Saturday morning when I walked into Athens, Ohio, an idyllic college town and the home of Ohio University, a couple of days later. I noticed a 30 pack of beer sitting directly in the middle of the road as I got into town. I laughed loudly upon seeing it and stopped to check it out, all without realizing that I was in danger of disturbing the sleep of a particular young gentleman nearby. There was a couch on the small lawn of one of the many houses that lined the street next to me, and this young fellow was sleeping on it just a few feet away. The morning dew had settled on his thin blanket. He grunted and rolled over, his face burying into the corner of the damp couch. I whispered out a short apology and continued along my way.

A man bought me lunch at Casa Nueva, a unique Mexican restaurant in the heart of Athens that is owned as a co-op by most of its employees. The atmosphere inside the place was laid back. It felt more like a coffee shop than a bar/restaurant. Nobody there was dressed up, and lots of people had long hair and beards. As we sat at the bar and chatted, the man who bought me lunch said, "Yeah, man, went to school here like 30 years ago and never bothered to leave." I wasn't surprised to hear this. There was an aura of unity that seemed to be present everywhere I explored in Athens. It felt progressive and youthful. Leaving would be tough for anyone, myself included.

I walked down a red brick street after leaving Casa Nueva. A blooming pear tree dropped white petals on the sidewalk. The sun was shining and spring had clearly arrived. Everyone smiled and said hello to me. A couple of guys with ratty dreadlocks and tattoos rolled cigarettes outside a cafe and asked if I wanted one.

People stopped every few minutes to offer me a ride as I made my way west out of town in the late afternoon. Right on the edge of Athens, a long-haired young man slowed his vehicle down to a stop in the road, said hello, and lobbed an apple to me out of his car window as he drove away. He threw up a peace sign, which I returned.

~

A bit further down Ohio Route 56, the sun was dipping down and I found myself in the familiar situation of having no idea where I was going to sleep. The road became curvy and weaved through hills of all sizes, farms sat peacefully in the narrow valleys created by them. Almost all of the land around the road was fenced, which made me hesitant to trespass. As I worried about this and munched on some Pop Tarts, I saw a sign just ahead for a game preserve of some kind. It seemed like a promising lead.

I walked up the dirt road to what I thought was the office for the preserve, but nobody was there. It was well past closing time. There was a sign that read: NO OVERNIGHT CAMPING. After spinning around in frustration, I noticed a house up the road a bit through the trees and could tell that the vehicle in its driveway was a Forest Service truck, so I proceeded to check it out. The fear of not having a place to sleep made me much more bold than usual. As I approached the rustic but clean looking two story house, dog barks erupted from all directions. So much for a quiet arrival.

Life On Foot

    I knocked on the front door. No answer. I knocked again and waited. Nothing. As I was sulking my way back down the road, the side door of the house creaked open and a young boy who looked to be about ten years old stuck his head out and simply said, "Hi."
    I said, "Hey man! Any chance your parents are home?"
    "Mom! Someone's here!" his high-pitched voice cried into the house. A minute or so later, a short, good looking lady in a sweatshirt, jeans, and tall rubber rain boots came out the door and said, "Can I help you?" She had a groggy look in her eyes and appeared to have been napping.
    "Yeah, my name is Nate, I'm walking across America and looking for a place I might be able to camp tonight. I saw the no camping sign for the preserve, but with the Forest Service truck up here I figured I'd ask someone directly. Is that your truck?"
    "Nope, it's my husband's, but we can go see him. He's usually does things pretty much by the book, but he might make an exception," she said. Her name was Helen. She had a German accent that was nice to listen to. I got into Helen's car and we made our way to the family farm just a few minutes down the road.
    We got there and found her husband, Dave, working on something just over a short hill behind the barn. I did my best to look as normal as possible, which always proved to be difficult when I was so dirty and scared all the time. I could tell that he was a bit apprehensive at first, and wondering who the homeless dude was that just shown up with his wife, but after explaining what I was doing there, he warmed up to the dirty beggar that was me. Dave was a tall and handsome guy with glasses and short black hair. He was wearing overalls and

sweating from whatever manual labor he was doing over the hill.

I was soon inside the farm's barn meeting the horses and barn cats. "Our house is full, but you're welcome to sleep here in the barn. We've got a nice tack room. We'll take you back to the house, you can take a shower, and have dinner with us, then we'll bring you back to sleep for the night. In the morning, we'll pick you up for a nice big breakfast at the house," Helen said.

On the drive back to the house, Helen explained her and Dave's mission with the farm. They wanted to become almost completely self-sufficient in the next few years and to live more simply. Helen had a peaceful way about her, but she wasn't afraid of hard work. At the barn she had been moving hay bales, lugging water buckets around, shoveling out the horse pens, and breaking a good sweat, all in her floppy rubber boots. She loved her horses and had a soft spot for shelter dogs as well. There were at least five dogs at the house.

I hung out with Helen and Dave's young son, Michael, for quite a while. He was energetic in the way kids are, and was practically begging for me to join him outside to play around. Helen kept saying, "Nate, you don't have to go out there, you can just relax if you want." What she didn't realize was that although I was 22, at heart I was about 10, so Michael was doing a bit more convincing than was actually necessary to get me out the door.

We hung out in Michael's little fort. We shot wooden elastic guns at each other. We shot BB guns at cans. We shot a bow and arrow at a hay bale. We shot everything that could be shot. He beat me in every shooting competition we had and made sure to let me know just how poorly I was doing at every opportunity. He did this in the unknowingly condescending way that young kids do when they're kicking your ass at something. He said things like, "Oh, well that was close, maybe next time," "That was pretty good, want to try again?" and "Maybe if you keep practicing you can beat me someday."

Hanging out with Michael was like hanging out with myself when I was his age. It was an enjoyable little flashback to my own BB gun and bow and arrow shooting days back in central Maine.

Dinner was fantastic, and a shower not only cleaned off my hiker stench, but also eased my aching muscles and bones. Back in the barn later that night, I laid out my sleeping back on a cot in the tack room. After poking my head out the door to say goodnight to the horses, I drifted off to sleep to the muffled sound of twangy folk music coming from a dusty barn radio, left on 24 hours a day to entertain my equine roommates.

~

I met Ken and Adele through Helen and Dave, and was invited to stay with them for a couple days. They lived near Hocking Hills State Park in a heavily wooded area surrounded by deep caves, bubbling streams, and hidden waterfalls. The terrain approaching Hocking Hills reminded me a lot of home in certain places. Curvy two-lane roads cut between, as well as directly up and over, medium sized hills that never seemed to end. Up and down I went. I saw lots of little farms. The grass was getting greener by the day. I wore shorts for the first time after leaving Dave and Helen's home. My pasty legs had a bit of catching up to do when it came to rivaling the noticeable tan that I had already gotten on my face and parts of my arms.

After walking up an impossibly steep hill, I arrived at Ken and Adele's house. It was the kind of hill that was steep and irritating enough to make me want to turn around and go right home, but getting there turned out to be well worth the extra work. I was told that their home could be identified by the blue bottle trees in the yard. I didn't quite know what that meant, but figured that blue bottle trees would be hard to miss. After feeling like I had gone too far and missed their house for quite some time, I walked around one last curve in the road, and a short tree with blue bottles on its branches came into view.

The house was well aged and full of character, a simple saltbox farmhouse built in the 1890s. Little knick knacks, quirky lawn ornaments, and rocks of all sizes were spread around. It wasn't messy looking, and each piece had clearly been placed with intent. There was a small garden. Lots of blue glass bottles were placed on the end of sticks that were stuck into the ground and on each branch of that short tree in the yard – the same tree that had let me know that I was at the right house.

I approached the open front door of the house and Adele came out to greet me. She was petite with curly blondish hair she kept pulled back. Her smile and warm, friendly eyes made me feel welcome instantly. There was usually a certain degree of awkwardness when I would meet someone who had volunteered to let me stay in their home for the first time. When someone does such a thing, you basically glide through all of the small-talk-getting-to-know-each-other stuff quickly and find yourself injected directly into their lives — a stranger who magically appears in their daily routines. But with Adele it was different. I felt like I had known her for years. And it all made perfect sense. She was a storyteller by profession. Her job was to draw people in with her eyes, facial expressions, and gentle yet attention-grabbing voice. She traveled and told stories, usually to groups of school children, as well as at local fairs. When I learned what she did for work, it made the whimsical design of the yard and house seem appropriate. It looked like a place where a storyteller would live. I soon met Ken, Adele's husband. Ken was handsome, tall, and thin, and always wore a slight smile when he talked, which made it seem like he was about to burst out laughing any second.

Ken and Adele were spiritual people. Our conversations carried on for hours about all things life, death, ceremony, religion, prayer, and meditation. These conversations were paired with walks in the woods. We explored secluded waterfalls far out into the surrounding forests that only a handful of people knew about. We also visited Ash Cave. The rim of Ash Cave spans about 700 feet, its depth measures in at about 100 feet. A waterfall ran over the edge of the cave, landing in a rocky pool that stood out from the otherwise sandy cave bottom. Hemlock trees hung precariously over the edge of its mossy walls.

There were times when we would be talking and Adele would launch directly into telling a story without me even knowing it. Several minutes later, I'd be dumbfounded and amazed at what I was hearing, then she would say some barely noticeable thing that would make me wonder if the whole thing was made up. Adele expertly blurred the line between what was really happening and an imaginary world of her own creation. There was no rest for the weary mind around her.

As we talked one day, Adele told me about ancient aboriginal civilization known as the Picts. She said that the Picts resided in the Misty Isles long ago. They were known for being fierce in battle, both men and women, and for covering themselves in bright blue paint before fighting. They were short, strong, and had long and wild looking, frazzled hair.

Nobody could contain them militarily, including the Romans, until finally the Scots subdued the Picts and took them captive. Over generations the Scots and Picts mated, causing the lines between the two groups to be blurred, and after many years these descendants migrated to the mountains of Appalachia.

She said that if I saw any little women around with bushy hair who liked talking and arguing just for the sake of arguing, that they might be one of the descendants. But, to be sure that she was a Pict/Scottish descendant and not just Scottish, you had to check her kitchen cabinet. If it held a set of blue dishes, she surely was one of them.

As I listened and thought about this, Adele went quiet and slowly looked toward her own set of blue dishes sitting on a nearby shelf. My eyes followed hers and everything came together. She was good.

~

During the 20 miles between Williamsport and Morrow, Ohio, I hurriedly walked, ran, threw tantrums during which I slammed my walking sticks to the ground and screamed at the sky, obsessively checked the time, skipped snacks and meals to save precious minutes, and got a short ride from an old hippie in a rustbucket of a van.

All of this was done to accomplish one goal: to get to the Morrow post office before it closed.

And believe it or not, I made it with two minutes to spare. After getting the package waiting there for me, which contained my new and very much needed tent, I pleaded, "Can you *please* give me just a minute to throw my old tent in a package and get it out. I can't be carrying two tents," to the perturbed looking woman behind the counter.

"I'm sorry, no," she replied with an unenthused look, and then slid the metal CLOSED gate down over the service window.

"Thank you for being so helpful," I said and walked out.

I stomped angrily back toward the road with my new tent held under one arm and my other arm holding both of my walking sticks. I dropped one of my sticks and yelled and kicked and screamed like an infant.

After trudging up the road for a few minutes, I noticed an impressive house to my right. What caught my attention about it was the dog in the yard. I thought that it was a Boxer at first glance, which reminded me of my dog back home, so I stopped to watch as the playful pup wandered across the lawn. It was at this point that something took over me. The next thing I knew, I was walking up the long driveway toward the house and intending to ask the owner if I could camp in the field behind their property.

I don't really know why I chose to do this. It wasn't like finding a place to sleep was urgent. The day was still relatively young. Even if it had been a more urgent situation, there was an overgrown field with plenty of cover just past the house that I could easily have hidden away in. But I was going to knock on this door, and I truly did not know why. If I had to take a guess as to why I picked the house, I would say that it was possibly my need to say hello to and wrestle/cuddle with every cute dog I see that drew me there. I saw the dog in the yard and immediately launched into a must-play-with-doggie trance. These are a common event during my day-to-day life.

I got to the house's tall wooden door and knocked. There was some movement on the other side of it. Quite a few seconds passed, then a lady opened the door just wide enough to peek her head out and said, "How can I help you?"

How can *she help me? What am I doing here?*

"Ahh, umm, I have sort of a weird question for you. My name is Nate, I'm walking across the U.S. from coast to coast. I noticed your field and was wondering if I might be able to set up my tent out there and get some rest for the night. I'll be gone early in the morning," I said.

She didn't seem to think about it at all and replied, "Sure, go ahead and set your stuff up over there," while motioning over to a tall line of trees on the edge of her property. She answered so quickly that it almost seemed like she had been expecting me to show up.

I heard a yell from the house right as I got my tent set up. "Hey! Come in here and get something to eat!"

On sore feet thanks to the day's extra strain because of the race to the Post Office, I limped through two small garden plots and across a perfectly cut lawn to the house, then made my way through a side door into the kitchen. The place was gorgeous. It had high ceilings with 200 year old wood beams exposed, a shiny hardwood floor, and finely crafted cabinets. The dog that had grabbed my attention from the road just a few minutes earlier joyfully smacked his tail off the table repeatedly as I patted his head. His name was Buster.

Buster's human was Maureen. She seemed confused as to why she was feeding a stranger and letting him camp on her property, all while her husband just happened to be out of town and she was home alone. I was confused as to why I had so randomly chosen to knock on her door. Confusion reigned.

Maureen rattled off a long string of questions about the walk and myself. She pried deeper and deeper in the 'why' behind my trek. I still had no real idea why I had chosen to stop there, but I quickly realized why she had allowed me to stay. Being a writer and a blogger, she was interested in stories, and the grubby hobo who came knocking for a place to sleep was sure to have some. She just couldn't let me leave without knowing more. It was fortunate that she found my homelessness interesting and worthy of a conversation instead of a call to the police department. We talked for at least two hours as Maureen fed me bowl after bowl of chicken noodle soup and all kinds of other goodies.

I took the following day off at the house, where I enjoyed multiple hot showers, ate like a king, watched TV, played/wrestled/cuddled with Buster, and most importantly made a great new friend in Maureen. While enjoying a meal at Maureen's favorite Thai restaurant on my second day there, I sadly realized that not only was my time in Morrow winding down, but my time in the Buckeye State was as well. A couple more days and I would be crossing the Ohio River into northern Kentucky. The acute sadness that I felt when leaving a place always surprised me. I should have been excited to advance westward and leave these places behind in the dust, but I rarely was.

As we ate, Maureen told me that all sorts of wanderers would often show up at her home unexpectedly when she was a kid. Her parents fed them and helped in any way they could, but couldn't understand why they kept coming. What they didn't know was that their home was marked. Even today in some places, hobos and other types of transient folks will often leave marks on sidewalks, trees, or signs near the homes of kind people, as well as those who should be avoided. There is an entire language of hobo signs. This was interesting to think about as I pondered why I had chosen to stop there for really no reason at all, other than the fact that I felt I should. Perhaps some old hobo spirits were pushing me Maureen's way.

    I looked up some hobo signs later on and thought the one for "Kindhearted Lady" would best describe Maureen. For whatever reason, it was a small smiling cat. I really should have carved it into the telephone pole at the end of her driveway.

Chapter 9: Best Easter Ever

The next stop was Cincinnati, where I unknowingly walked the outskirts of what had once been named the most dangerous neighborhood in America, a part of the city called Over The Rhine. I dodged prostitutes and groups of drug dealers that stood on corners with addicts circling around them like vultures. Luckily, no cute dogs presented themselves, as my must-play-with-doggie tendencies might not have landed me in a place as friendly as Maureen's.

The city treated me well once I hit the downtown area. I stayed with a CouchSurfing host named Ricky there. Ricky was passionate about a lot of things, one of them being thriftiness. He drove a beat up pickup truck that he bought for $200 or something like that off Craigslist. He was also an avid dumpster diver and almost never spent any money on groceries. He prepared a wonderful meal for the two of us entirely of food he had picked up out of a Trader Joe's dumpster.

Ricky wanted to take me dumpster diving one night, so we stayed up late for the occasion. I felt excited as we parked in front of a closed grocery store and turned on our headlamps. We approached our first set of dumpsters and Ricky said, "Ah, shit."

"What's the matter?" I asked.

"They locked it all up," he said as he tried to find a way to pry the dumpster's sliding doors open. Fat padlocks stood in the way of accomplishing this.

"That sucks," I replied.

"No big deal, really, I'll just come back and Gorilla Glue them," he noted quietly.

"What?"

"I'll put superglue in all the locks. Eventually they'll get tired of buying new locks and stop locking it," he said calmly as we hopped back in the truck and drove off. Ricky was quite a character.

I did my best to figure out the public transportation in Cincinnati the next morning, got to my starting point for the day, and made my way over the C. W. Bailey Bridge into Kentucky, The Bluegrass State.

~

A couple of days after entering Kentucky, it was Easter morning. I stood looking out the window of my hotel room in Florence in horror as a deluge of rain pounded the city. Ankle deep puddles were forming in the hotel parking lot. *How bad would they be on the side of the road?* The rain had lasted most of the previous afternoon's walk, during which I had gotten thoroughly soaked, and continued on through the night. I'd spent an hour in the hotel bathroom with a hair blow dryer trying to dry my sopping boots with little success.

As I looked out the hotel window while thinking about my impending doom, a loud vibration shook me out of my depression. My phone was ringing. It was Maureen from Ohio calling.

I answered the call. She said, "I'm going to come get you so you can have Easter lunch with my family."

"Ok!," I replied excitedly, "I know it's a long drive though, are you sure?"

"I'm coming to get you," she said back quickly. Maureen was all business, as usual. About forty-five minutes later, she was at the hotel. I hustled out to her car under my umbrella, threw my stuff in its back seat, and just like that we were off to Cincinnati. Easter had never meant much to me before, but on that day it became important. I was feeling lonely that morning as I stared out the window into the rain. Families were gathering, kids were looking for decorated eggs and candy treasures, lazy Sundays were being enjoyed. And there I was, about to get soaked to the bone and cold all by myself.

We arrived in Cincinnati, where Maureen's family welcomed me in right in. Maureen put me to work in the kitchen. She laughed quietly to herself as I struggled to cut and mix even the most basic ingredients. We all enjoyed a large meal and everyone retired to the living room area afterward. I dozed off in a comfy rocking chair for a few minutes. I had gotten to enjoy a lazy Sunday after all.

Maureen drove me all the way back to Florence in the early afternoon. The rain had subsided for the most part, and I was thankful for the scattered rays of sun that were poking through the still cloudy sky. I took one last look at the tall red and white striped water tower in the middle of the city that read "FLORENCE Y'ALL" and made my way down U.S. Route 42.

A couple of hours later, I was walking through a quiet neighborhood when I heard a yell coming from behind me. "Hey! Hold on a second thurr, buddeh!" Turning around, I saw a man running across his lawn to catch up to me. Once he did he said, "Where ya headed?" After explaining the walk, he replied, "Well, come over and have an Easter meal with us, we've got plenty of food." I had gone from a morning of despair to not just one, but two Easter meals.

The man who chased me down on the road was named Steve. Steve and his son were strongly religious and still dressed in their Sunday best late into the afternoon. It was the first time I'd ever seen "Christians" smoke cigarettes. *It must be a Southern thing* I thought as they breathed out lingering billows of smoke into the humid Kentucky air. They went on and on about "the Lawd" and inquired as to whether or not I "knew Jesus Chraahst as my savyah." Everything sounded so Southern to me as a born and raised Yankee.

Their family was large and the Easter dinner portions were sized accordingly. Various types of barbequed meat, probably the second best macaroni and cheese I'd ever had (nobody beats my grandmother's), and heaps of baked beans were carefully piled onto styrofoam plates. In between platefuls everyone sat around on the porch, while an assortment of kids ran around in the yard. I tossed a ball around with the youngest boy of the bunch until his lessening attention span drew him elsewhere.

Speaking of attention spans, my feet and mind, both conditioned for perpetual movement, were ready to hit the highway. The setting sun was essentially the only indicator that affected my goings-on during the day and it had already been lowering itself steadily for some time. I made hints for about 15 minutes in several conversations about the uncertainty surrounding my sleeping arrangements, all with no luck in terms of picking up a camping lead or an invitation to set up shop on the back lawn of the house. Saying thank you all around to my new friends, I ambled across a lawn so green that I felt uncomfortable walking on it and was soon back on the cracked and familiar pavement.

I found myself at a peculiar fork in the road with about an hour of daylight left. To my left was a patch of woods that I could easily find a place to camp in. To my right was a road that led to a state park, which had the potential to contain showers and a covered camping area. The park was four miles off my route, but would be well worth the added mileage if I could stay dry through the night and get a hot shower. There was no phone service available for calling the park to see if they actually offered these things, but I decided to take the gamble anyway.

About two miles down the side road the rain started pouring furiously out of the dark, saturated clouds above. Shortly after the rain started, the sun went down completely and I was walking in cold, wet darkness. A car narrowly missed hitting me. I had to dive over a guardrail to avoid the collision.

I arrived at the state park in an hour or so. After terrifying a clean-cut looking family when I walked out of the dark abyss to their tarp covered site to ask where the campground office was, I made my way to the fifth wheel camper where the campground host was staying. I knocked twice on the door and snapped the skinny old man inside out of his cable TV induced stupor, and he stomped over to the door. Standing in the rain, I asked, "Any chance I could set up my tent under that covered picnic area?" as I pointed to the nearby picnic pavilion that offered the only real shelter on the grounds. "I've walked a long way to get here and just want to stay dry tonight, I'm already soaked," I added, hoping to garner an ounce of sympathy out of the man.

"Sorry, but I can't let ya do that, and it's $25 a night. Make sure to leave it in an envelope before you head out," he said with a scowl and promptly shut the door in my face.

Without wanting to waste the energy required to convince him to change his mind, I turned around without saying a word and walked over to the dimly lit cinder block building that housed the campground bathrooms. I had a plan. This plan involved setting my tent up in the bathroom, putting the rain fly on it, somehow dragging it out into the still pouring rain, staking the damn thing down, and then transporting my things back and forth from the bathroom to the tent one small load at a time under the cover of my already soaked rain jacket and umbrella. It was a nightmare, but I wasn't overly stressed. The road was slowly changing me in a way that allowed me to transform misfortune into something, anything positive. I knew that eventually, when all was said and done and the skies had cleared, I'd have yet another good story to tell.

Sopping wet and exhausted after the ordeal of getting to the campground and setting up my tent, I snuggled up inside my sleeping bag to eat the ham sandwiches Maureen had sent me off with and drink my last can of Coke. Somehow I was still hungry, even after the day's set of huge meals. The faint, orange light from the bathroom building illuminated the inside of my tent just enough so I could see as I ate. I sipped on my Coke and listened to the constant pattering of raindrops all around me, enjoying the leftovers from the best Easter of my life.

~

Not long after the best Easter ever it was time to cross the Ohio River into Indiana. The bridge that I was supposed to use for this crossing was roaring with traffic. It seemed like it was too big to be legal for pedestrians to cross. As I stood next to the bridge's off-ramp and considered what to do, I noticed a police car driving down it toward me. I waved him down, and he pulled over. "Is it legal to walk across this bridge?" I asked through the cruiser's rolled down window.

"Honestly, I really don't know. My guess would be that you can't," the officer replied.

"Are you going to arrest me if I do?" I asked.

"Nope, go for it," he said with a laugh and drove away. So I crossed the bridge and was in Indiana.

Chapter 10: Southern Indiana Celebrity

A few miles outside of Madison, Indiana, I got an all too familiar sinking feeling in my gut. I couldn't find an adequate place to camp. Tall hills much too steep for a tent rose up from the road to my right. To my left, the Ohio River was bloated from the heavy rainfall over the previous couple of weeks. It encroached on riverside homes and cabins, some of which had been almost completely submerged by the flooding. Basketballs, lawn furniture, and trash bobbed up and down in the murky water and floated steadily south toward Louisville.

While worrying about this and leaning on a guardrail to have a snack and water break, I suddenly remembered a piece of advice that I'd gotten a while back from a fellow cross-country walker. His advice had been to call the local police department dispatch when I was heading into a town, and to ask them if there was anywhere that I could camp safely and legally. According to him it worked almost every time and most police departments and officers were actually enthusiastic about the idea of a cross-country walk. I hadn't tried this strategy since the very first night of the walk back in Delaware. If you remember, my inquiry was immediately denied when I did. I think I had just figured that it would never work and forgotten about it.

Excited about this new option for finding a place to rest my head, I took my phone out, Googled the Madison Indiana Police Department, and found their phone number. Then I froze.

One of the reasons I think some people back home probably doubted that I'd actually do the walk was because I was very shy. And if there was one thing I hated, it was calling people I didn't know on the phone. Hell, I didn't even like calling people I *did* know. Awkward and shy was my thing. But if I wanted to make it across the unforgiving continent in front of me, I needed to change that, whether I really wanted to or not.

As the phone was ringing, I walked up the overgrown driveway of an abandoned house to get away from the noisy road and river. "Hello, Madison Police Department," said the voice on the other end.

I explained what I was doing in a horrendously ineloquent manner and the response that I received was a typical one.

"You're walking?" the lady on the phone asked.

"Yes, should be in Madison in about an hour," I replied.

"Let me ask an officer and see what I can do," she said kindly.

Cue the on hold music...

"Sir, come to the police department when you get here and we'll figure something out for you."

"THANK YOU SO MUCH!" I shrieked into the phone. Feeling renewed, I practically skipped the remaining few miles into Madison, a town tucked carefully in between the Ohio River and hills coated in flourishing forests.

~

Once I got through the rather mundane east side of Madison, I wandered into a true American Main Street setting. Two and three story brick buildings lined the streets. The fronts of the buildings were neatly painted with pastels that were soft, but distinct. They burst with intensity against the old brick. The old buildings had been reconditioned to house modern shops and cafes.

What struck me most as I moved down a squeaky clean downtown sidewalk was that there were virtually no vacant storefronts to be found in Madison. Typically in small town America, where most towns are dying a slow but steady death, a quarter or more of the storefronts on any given Main Street are abandoned, going out of business, or have ugly FOR RENT signs in their dusty, dark windows. Madison, on the other hand, was overflowing with activity, much like its flooded neighbor, the Ohio River.

Arriving at the police station on Main Street, I walked in and explained to an attendant behind a bulletproof glass window who I was. An officer soon came out and greeted me with a finger-crushing grip. We talked about my trip and he said, "Well, we'd love to help you, how about you just set up your tent right out there in the parking lot between those two cars. There's an empty slot right there for you." One of the cars was a Toyota Camry and the other a Jeep Cherokee. He walked me out into the parking lot, pointed me in the direction of the public restroom building down the street, and went back into the station. I had found my parking spot for the night.

As I was getting settled in I looked up to notice the sky was turning a dark shade of gray. I only had a few minutes to spare before the seemingly daily downpouring of rain began soaking everything in sight. One gets very talented at predicting weather when they are abused by the worst it has to offer on a constant basis. Hustling to get my home together, I hopped in just as the first drops started to fall. With gun toting, highly trained officers of the law roaming around ready to pick off any intruder intent on ruining my night's sleep, I dozed off without a care in the world.

The early morning sun woke me out of my dreamless sleep. Outside of my normal walk, eat, walk some more, eat some more, sleep, do it all over again agenda, there was a new bit of excitement on the docket for this sunny April day. I was going to be getting a new pair of boots.

My trusty Merrells had put in around 1,200 miles of hiking both on the walk and during previous treks into the New England mountains. As much as I wanted to avoid it, they needed to be retired. I had noticed a small business on my way into Madison the previous evening called Hertz Shoe Store, and decided that it would be the best place to go to find their replacement. Arriving before they opened, I sat around for about 15 minutes before someone showed up. She was an older lady, and I got the impression that she was the owner of the place. Being that she was working alone, I helped her move a few tables that needed rearranging in the store, then started browsing through the available boot choices. I had considered getting shoes, but boots were an old habit that I wasn't yet ready to break.

A pair of Keen hiking boots caught my eye, so I promptly tried them on for size. They felt like pillows compared to my ripped and weathered Merrells. I said, "Yup, these are the ones!" and plopped them up on the counter to pay. Not that the boots were uncomfortable in any way, but this is a good illustration of how much I hate shopping. I had just made a decision about a piece equipment that was arguably the most important possession I owned and one that I would be wearing day in and day out for at least the next 1,000 miles of walking in under two minutes, all without doing any prior research. There is a high probability that even if they had not been comfortable, I still would have just bought them anyway for the sake of ending my shopping responsibilities as soon as possible.

I headed up Main Street once again to the building that housed the public restroom, water fountains and a few drink machines. The new boots felt good on their first real test run under Wilson's weight. I sat down on one of the benches in the building and stared at my old, raggedy boots. The attachment that I felt to them was surprising. It felt like I was saying goodbye to an old friend as I placed them carefully into a trash can.

Just after I finished saying goodbye to my old Merrells, a lady came in the door and asked what I was doing. Wilson had once again caught someone's attention as he leaned so seductively against the bench.

I'm walking across America, yadda, yadda, yadda.

"Well, if you're in Madison, you just *have to* go to Hinkle's. Best little burgers you've ever had. Here are a couple Hinkle's Bucks, go get yourself something to eat."

She handed me three green bills, each worth one "Hinkle Burger Buck" and "Good for buying stuff at Hinkle's." I decided to act on her suggestion immediately, so I crossed the street and began walking up to Hinkle's.

Opened by Winfred Hinkle in 1933 and still in its original location on Main Street, Hinkle's is the definition of a local landmark. I easily spotted the can't-miss Hinkle's sign, which jutted out over the sidewalk and lured in hungry shoppers and passers by. There were a couple of different dining areas inside, one of them being a diner style counter. I opted for the other choice, which was a small room with a newly waxed, black and white checkered floor. The tables had a classic diner look — immaculately clean, black tops with polished chrome trim.

I ordered four burgers. They were White Castle-like small burgers served by default with pickles and grilled onions. They arrived in front of me within just a few minutes of ordering and I dug right in. They were perfect. A flawless blend of greasy beef, pickles, onions, and a soft steamed bun. I easily could have put away a dozen of them. The burgers and a side order of fries were gone before I even knew what happened.

Wanting to keep one of my Hinkle Burger Bucks as a keepsake, I paid my cheerful waitress with a combination of the little bit of cash that I had left and my two remaining Hinkle Bucks, then began heaving Wilson toward the door. A lady sitting at one of the tables in the back of the restaurant asked, "Whatcha doin' with that backpack?" as I was doing this.

I turned around. "Walking to California. Just passing through Madison right now. What a great town!"

"That's neat, do ya carry a gun?" It was a common question.

"Nope, just a small knife and my walking sticks, so far so good."

"You're crazy! I'd be carryin a gun if I were—"

"She's got one, and believe me she'll use it!" the man sitting across from her at the table, who was either her husband or boyfriend, shouted out. He looked at me and rolled his eyes.

"Oh yeah?" I said, wanting to know more about what he meant, but unsure if I should dig any deeper into the story behind his remark. It turned out I didn't need to ask.

The lady said, "Well, one day I came home and caught him lookin' at somethin' dirty on the computer. I'd already told him he couldn't do that anymore. So I

reached in my purse, grabbed my pistol, and walked right up to that damn computer and shot the screen."
"Crazy, right?" he exclaimed.
"At least I didn't shoot at *yeeeoouuu!*" she shouted back, "Jim's wife shot *aaat* him through a door when they were fightin'! Remember that?"
"Ayup," he replied quietly, apparently feeling fortunate that he at least wasn't poor ol' Jim. The matter seemed to be settled. They both went back to their meals like nothing in the conversation was out of the ordinary, so I said goodbye and got back out onto Main Street.

~

Down Highway 56 was French Lick, a small town with an attention-grabbing name that I was eager to explore. Growing up a Boston Celtics fan in New England, Larry Bird, also affectionately known as "The Hick From French Lick," was a hero of mine. Bird had grown up in French Lick and even lived there during and after his days in the NBA. Visiting French Lick became a sort of pilgrimage because of this. I had wanted to visit the place since I was a young kid. When my route took on a more southern tone after getting lost in Pennsylvania and turning back to Maryland, I knew exactly where I was going to aim for in Indiana.

Prior to crossing over from Kentucky into Indiana, I knew almost nothing about French Lick except for the fact that Larry Legend had grown up there. I'd seen the movie *Hoosiers* a bunch of times, and figured that it was probably a lot like the town in that film, which had inspired stereotypes (some true, some not) of Indiana folks for decades. It wasn't until I reached Vevay, some 95 miles east of French Lick, that I learned the town was actually home to a world-class resort and casino. The public relations people at the French Lick Resort had learned about my walk from a local newspaper and offered me a free room for a night. I accepted their generous offer and looked forward to a night of luxury.

From Paoli, a town about eight miles east of French Lick on 56, I took the longest ride of the walk up to that point. Water had taken over several parts of the road I was supposed to be walking on. The severe flooding that had been following me since Washington D.C. was wreaking havoc on many communities in the area. A good part of downtown French Lick was under a couple feet of water. This seemed to be a huge problem for me, until a reporter from the Paoli Times newspaper was kind enough to transport me through the flood zone. He ended up writing a story about my trip titled "Walker Gets Soggy Local Welcome During His Coast-To-Coast Journey," which was published a few days later.

I was shocked when I arrived at the resort. The place was enormous. I had been camping in the woods and staying in $30 motel rooms full of cigarette smoke damage and mystery stains for months, and felt instantly overwhelmed just by the sight of it. This was compounded even more as I met Dyan and Tessa, the two ladies from the public relations department at the resort who would be showing me around, and numerous other staff members who all seemed interested in the walk and excited to meet me. I awkwardly posed for a few photos in the lobby of the main building, and then was treated to a delicious lunch.

There were two hotel buildings on the resort grounds — French Lick Springs and West Baden Springs. I would be staying at French Lick Springs. The building towered over the surrounding landscape. It had a bright and inviting yellow-gold brick exterior. The windows were trimmed with white paint. A long white porch with lots of rocking chairs on it stretched along the front of the building. West Baden Springs was just down the road, a stunning building in its own right.

The first real heyday of the resort was during Prohibition. Over a dozen illegal casinos and speakeasies found their way into the small towns of French Lick and West Baden during the time. These illicit, smoke filled hangouts offered gambling and bootleg booze to the some of the country's most elite public figures. Once the visitors to these establishments got their fills of their favorites vices, they would retire to their suites at their hotel of choice. Some of these casinos operated for decades, until a final raid by the government in 1949 forced the last of them out of commission.

The current French Lick building was constructed in 1901 after the original one, built in 1845, was lost in a fire. The resort thrived for decades, but gradually began falling out of its original state of grandeur during the 1970s, and continued to decline into the early 2000s. An answer to the resort's problems finally came in 2005 when William Cook, one of the richest men in America, backed most of a massive restoration project that renovated the French Lick grounds, as well as almost completely reconstructed the nearby West Baden Hotel.

After walking into the lobby of the French Lick building and meeting everyone, I took a look around. A flight of marble stairs guided guests up to the second floor, which was visible through a balcony overlooking the lobby. The ceiling in the lobby showcased colorful and detailed fresco style artwork, with chandeliers illuminating it and the lobby below. Italian mosaic floors and marble columns clashed beautifully against the endless variety of luminous golden designs and artwork. It was actually difficult to take it all in. It was magnificent. Too magnificent for a dirty hiker like myself.

Arriving at my room, the yellow-gold theme from the outside of the building continued there, giving it a bright feel that was only amplified by its tall windows and open layout. I never wanted to leave.

After a full afternoon of relaxation and thinking I could really get used to being in such a place, hunger drew me down to the 1875 Steakhouse, one of the fine dining options for French Lick guests. The meal was on the resort's tab, which clearly made me excited, but I really had no idea what I was getting myself into. To start, my grimy hiker garb was completely inappropriate for dining in a world-class resort. My gray, sweat stained tee shirt, zip-off shorts, and sandals didn't quite fit in with the luxurious theme of the restaurant and the finest fancy dinner attire worn by the restaurant's other guests. I appreciated the hostess' attempt to not laugh as I hesitantly approached her and said, "Hey, I had a reservation for a table. It's just me."

People stared as I tried to sneak by without being noticed on the way to my table. After the seemingly never-ending walk there, I sat down and enjoyed some people watching out a nearby window. By people watching out a nearby window, I really mean I was just trying to avoid making any eye contact with the nicely dressed folks who were glancing at me from every direction.

The waitress in charge of helping me came over and handed me a menu. Her name was Mary. My ridiculous appearance piqued her curiosity, so she asked what I was doing in French Lick. The walk was explained, and Mary then became more of a friend than just a waitress for my remaining time at the restaurant. Whenever there was a lull in her waitressing duties, she came over to my table to talk with me. It made being an underdressed lone diner in a restaurant full of dapper couples and groups much more enjoyable than it otherwise would have been.

I stared at the menu that Mary handed me in awe. I was so used to eating Chef Boyardee ravioli out of a can and peanut butter and jelly sandwiches that items such as jumbo lump crab cakes, lobster bisque, and filet mignon were nearly too much to even comprehend. And the prices. Oh, the prices. They weren't absurd for a restaurant of that caliber, but an entree cost what I would normally spend on five days worth of food. This made me hesitant to order, which Mary noticed. She helped me by saying, "Remember, it's on the resort! Get whatever you want."

Whatever I want? Was I dreaming? Ok then, let's do this.

Salad was sent out to me. Then a heaping dish of steamed asparagus. Then diver scallops with saffron infused couscous and curried tomato coulis. I didn't even know what most of those words meant, but they sounded tasty. This was all followed by a plate-filling piece of cheesecake with strawberry and pineapple topping. It was a meal of epic proportions. Fat and barely able to move, I got up and said goodbye to Mary. She handed me an envelope.

"What's this?"

"Just a gift from the staff. I went around and everybody put a little something in there for you and signed it," she said. Surprised and moved by such a kind gesture, I told her she could not possibly understand how much it meant to me. Getting back to my room, I opened up the envelope to find $30 in cash inside it, along with a short written message from everyone on staff that evening from chefs to waitresses.

Dyan and Tessa showed me around town and took me to visit Larry Bird's boyhood home the following day. I stared reverently at the vacant one story house. The backboard that Bird had used to hone his skills as a kid was still hanging from the garage next to it. It was a holy place for any Celtics fan. Even Bird's teammates sometimes felt drawn to see the hallowed structure for themselves. One of these teammates was the NBA's most cherished seven-foot red-headed flower child, Bill Walton, who once made the trip to Bird's home not long after the Celtics won the 1986 NBA Championship. Before leaving at the end of his visit, Walton dug up some dirt from the front lawn and placed it in a jar for safekeeping. He then ceremoniously spread the dirt around the basketball court at his own home in San Diego.

Chipped paint and a slightly overgrown yard were indicators that the property had clearly seen better days and years. It all seemed so modest. It can be easy to forget that great things often come from meager beginnings. Bird grew up in the poorest county in Indiana. His mother worked multiple jobs at a time to support him and his five siblings. Crushing debt drove his father to suicide in 1975. The little house on Washington Street was both humble and humbling.

The surrounding neighborhood was sunny and noiseless in the weekday afternoon. Basketball's blue-collar superstar had traveled far. As a young man, Bird would have walked north for just under a mile to get to school from his home. The final turn of this journey would have been onto what is now Larry Bird Boulevard.

~

Tessa and her husband, Keegan, invited me to their home and then to a cookout with two of their friends, Dave and Christina. Keegan and Dave took me out to shoot AR-15 and SKS assault rifles and a couple different shotguns. We drank beer and blasted targets with bullets. It was all quite manly.

I also visited an off-the-wall place called the French Lick Antique Hair Museum. This museum was located inside Body Reflections, a hair salon on Maple Street in downtown French Lick, and run by Tony Kendall.

Tony really loved hair. Along the walls of his salon were shelves packed neatly with items such as antique and vintage combs, scissors, razors, brushes, curling irons, and just about any other hair related item you could think of. The two most noticeable highlights of Tony's creation were a lock of Elvis Presley's hair and a wreath made entirely of human hair. The authenticated lock from the King of Pop attracted a lot of attention, but the wreath had most of my interest. It had belonged to some unidentified family. Over the course of many generations, members of this family had added sections of their own hair to the wreath, typically in the form of a delicately woven and detailed flower shape. I learned that hair wreathes were actually common family heirlooms during the Victorian era. Perfectly preserved in the frame, the hair looked as if it had just been cut, when really it hadn't been attached to a living human head for more than 100 years. I stood in the corner of Tony's salon and museum gazing at the wreath. It was morbid and beautiful.

Tony shook me out of my deep pondering about the hair wreath with an odd question. He wanted to know if he could cut off some of my hair. "Just a little snip," he said. The snip would be going straight into his "famous person" hair jar. A glass jar full of strands of hair from an indistinguishable amount of local celebrities and personalities sat on one of Tony's packed shelves, and I was about to be added to the mix. Tony and I posed for a photo, then he snapped his scissors and added a few strands of my hair to the jar.

Heading out of town on 56 after a couple of days and nights at the resort, a car pulled over to the side of the road ahead of me. A good looking young woman about my age got out of it. She said, "Are you the guy that's walking across America?"

"I'm one of them, anyway."

"I thought so, can I take a picture with you?"

I laughed. "Sure."

She got in close, held her cell phone out, took a photo, then said, "Bye!" and ran back over to her car and drove off.

Between the local newspapers, free meals and hotel rooms, people asking for photos with me, and my hair being put in a museum, I thought I was pretty hot stuff — nothing short of a southern Indiana celebrity. I thought about my newfound fame as I walked. It felt silly to be leaving the only place where people had ever thought I was a legitimately interesting person.

The road was not too busy, but pretty steep. As I topped the first big hill west of French Lick, I noticed a crappy little Toyota car coming down the road toward me. The car slowed down as it got close, and I waved at the man who was driving it. I thought he might be another one of my admirers wanting a photo. The man extended his arm fully as he clenched his fingers into a fist, then flipped up his middle finger. Back to reality.

~

Not too surprisingly, the rest of Indiana treated me well. Between French Lick and the Illinois border, some 80 miles of walking, I didn't spend any of my own money. People just handed me cash constantly, oftentimes without even introducing themselves. As always, taking money from strangers felt weird, but I took it anyway. Money buys food and I sort of needed that. Although I received help from lots of people, my main caretakers through that stretch were Helen and Brian Bruner.

I first met Helen and Brian when they offered to buy me lunch in a small town called Jasper. They had found me through the French Lick Resort's Facebook page, and I never turn down a free lunch. It's one of the more important core values I base my life upon. After a filling meal and enjoyable conversation with Helen and Brian, I made my way to a nearby Wal-Mart to stock up on groceries. While checking out, the man in front of me in line paid for everything I had, which was about $30 worth of food.

Helen then brought me dinner that same night in Huntingburg as I camped next to the baseball field where the movie *A League Of Their Own* was filmed. I had gone into the Wendy's in Huntingburg that afternoon for a snack, and someone there had bought my food for me and given me $20. Around Oakland City, a guy pulled over in a truck and gave me one of those survival bracelets made of parachute cord and an envelope with $30 in it. A couple of miles further down the road, a lady rolled down her window to give me a sandwich, a couple of oranges, and a soda.

    As I approached Princeton, Brian called and said there was already a hotel room reserved there for me. He had set it up in advance, and they were expecting my arrival. Two people then gave me $5 each as I walked through Princeton. I got to the hotel, and the two ladies at the front desk had made me a tray of cookies. They never even processed Brian's payment for the room, making my stay a free one. It was a borderline absurd streak of hospitality. I knew I would miss Indiana.

Chapter 11: Before The River Changed Paths

While walking down Illinois Route 1 on my first day in the Land of Lincoln, I noticed an old man hobbling as quickly as he could across his front lawn toward me. I took my headphones off and said hello to him. He said, "Didn't want ya walkin' by, saw you had those headphones on. What are you doin'?"

I told him about the walk. His name was Tom. He told me that he had terminal cancer and that he was just trying to enjoy whatever time he had left. I felt bad that he had run across his lawn just to get my attention. He was thin and frail looking, but seemed to be in a perfect mood.

Tom asked where I was sleeping that night, and I told him I didn't know. He was sweet and refused to quit until he found me a place to stay. He finally settled on calling a church up ahead in Keensburg, and the pastor there said I was welcome to come by. I told Tom that he had made my entire day. From the smile on his face, knowing he had helped me so much had made his too.

It took me about an hour to reach the church. I set up my tent on the lawn beside it and was promptly visited by the police. They had already gotten calls about me. As usual, they were kind and encouraging once they determined I wasn't dangerous.

The pastor of the church arrived shortly and invited me into his office to chat. I noticed a photo of someone in a military uniform on his desk and asked about it. It was one of his two sons. Both of them were in the military. The son in the photo had been killed in combat during a deployment in Iraq a couple of years earlier.

"Your son is a hero," I said.

He replied, "We like to think so."

~

Heading into the north side of Grayville on Route 1, I had one stop I was supposed to make. A guy named George was my connection there. I had been told I might be able to set up my tent near the fruit stand he owned.
Coming down North Court Street, I found George's fruit stand easily. With a name like Gone Bananas, it would have been hard to miss. The information I'd gotten about George proved to be helpful, except that it led me to believe that George owned only a fruit stand. George turned out to be a picker — a collector of anything he believed he could make a buck on, as well as some things he knew he couldn't, but decided to hold on to anyway. Washers and dryers sat for sale along with furniture, wholesale chips and candy, lawn mowers, and a variety of other items. You could even rent a U-Haul truck to transport everything home right there on the spot, because George had a truck rental business set up too.
George was short, round, wore glasses, had thinning white hair, and appeared to be in his fifties. He had moved to Grayville some years earlier on a hunch that his life's purpose was to start a food bank there. As George himself said to me, "God led me here." He ran the food bank for several years.
We talked for a while in the humid Illinois afternoon, and then George took me to meet a guy named Donny. Donny owned an auto repair business and gas station in Grayville. Killing a few minutes in the dusty waiting room of his shop, I bought a drink and looked around for all the things an auto repair shop

waiting room should have: outdated calendars, car posters, and a minimum of one wall clock that stopped working years earlier. Donny's shop had most of them. After a few minutes Donny walked in with a spring in his step as he wiped grease from his hands with a rag. Just as quickly as we had met, he said, "Let me buy you guys lunch. George, take him up to Chappy's. It's on me." As I have said, I never turn down a free lunch, so we headed over to Chappy's Bar And Grill from there.

After enjoying a tasty burger at Chappy's and getting to know George a bit more, I returned to Gone Bananas. I met Lana there, one of George's employees. Or maybe she wasn't, I never really understood the arrangement. Anyhow, Lana always hung out at the fruit stand and watched over the place while George zoomed around town trying to make a dent in his never-ending list of errands. Lana and I sat around and discussed the magic of the road. She had been homeless for years and technically still was. She had lived under bridges, slept under tarps, and hitchhiked. Although my level of homelessness had not quite approached what she had experienced, it was neat talking to someone who could relate to the nomadic, cheap lifestyle.

Lana and her husband, Scott, were living just outside of town at a campground in their fifth wheel camper. They were able to live there for free in exchange for doing odd jobs, such as mowing the campground lawns and emptying trash bins. With one rusty Ford Explorer between the two of them, no way to haul their home, Lana being technically unemployed, and Scott doing whatever short term jobs he could find around town while looking for something more permanent, they were struggling. Despite these circumstances, they were just as happy and optimistic as anyone. I was intrigued by Lana and her story and had to know more. When she invited me to stay at the campground with her and Scott, I responded with an immediate yes.

I spent most of the rest of the afternoon at the Grayville Public Library, where I had arranged with Lana for her and Scott to come pick me up at around 5 PM. I ventured out onto the library's front steps to make a phone call after being there for a bit. While talking to my mom back in Maine, a lady kept motioning over to me from the street a few parking spots down the curb. After telling my mom I'd call her back, I said, "Hey, everything ok?"

"I locked my keys in my car, *again*!" the lady said back in a frustrated tone, "Can I borrow your phone to call the police?" I handed her my phone and she called, only to be told that the police no longer offered car unlocking as a service. We stood on the sidewalk brainstorming for a few minutes, until I had the idea to go back to Donny's auto shop. Surely he would have the solution.

I ran around the corner and down the street, found Donny, and he made his way up to the lady's car with some device that could help her get into it. It took him just a few seconds to get it unlocked. The lady said, "What do I owe you?"

"Nothing, it's all set," Donny said with a smile as he headed back to his shop. People really looked out for each other in Grayville.

Lana arrived with Scott soon thereafter. I wasn't sure what to expect of Scott, but figured that he'd be an interesting fellow after hearing some of the things Lana told me about him. I walked down the steps of the library and there he was. He had long hair, was wearing a baseball hat, lugged around a big belly, and was rolling a cigarette as he leaned against his and Lana's

Explorer. He struck me as being highly intelligent once we began talking. The guy was sharp as a tack, which I must admit, I did not expect when I first saw him. He spoke with a slow, deliberate drawl that seemed almost aristocratic when paired with his well-structured and smooth way of putting thoughts together.

We arrived at the campground that Lana and Scott called home. I leaned Wilson against a rickety picnic table and went over to their camper. The campground was perched on top of a hill covered in tall trees. The forest canopy above was dense. Brown leaves from the previous fall still covered most of the ground.

Walking up to the camper, I was pleased to meet Duke the dog. Duke was a muscular, fawn colored Boxer. He looked like a beefier version of the dog Alana and I had shared back in Maine. I took a seat at a picnic table and Duke's massiveness overtook me. He put his paws up on my shoulders and gave me a kiss. The drool flying out of his drooping jowls was soon all over my face. "He doesn't usually like men, but he's takin' a real likin' to you," I heard Lana say between Duke's slobbery licks and happy grunts. I gave him a big hug and scratched behind his ears.

After taking a shower, it was time for dinner with Lana and Scott. I sat on the compact couch that lined one side of the surprisingly spacious inside of their camper. Scott sat directly in front of me in a recliner with its seat back and rolled a bunch of cigarettes. He balanced his hands on his basketball shaped, bare belly. Lana was in the tiny kitchen, cooking chicken and vegetable stir fry. In between stirring the contents of the pan, she came over and shared more of her stories with me.

Lana had experienced a lot of hardship, but was finally pulling things together. Her younger years had involved an abusive marriage, long periods of homelessness, and a couple of stints in jail. Her and Scott's previous house had been foreclosed on a few months back. Thankfully, they ended up scraping together just enough money to buy the camper.

    Lana remained unquestionably optimistic through it all. A slight smile never left her face. She always called me "hun" and "darlin'" and "sweetie." Living in a camper with no vehicle to move it, being unemployed, and barely getting by would be enough to sink the spirits of most people, but Lana knew what it was like to really have nothing. She was well aware of how fortunate she was to have a roof over her head and even enough food to make a stranger dinner. We talked about her vision for her and Scott's future as she cooked. Lana looked up from the stove and said, "You can't ever give up hope."

    It was a dinner I still cherish to this day. Being around such honest and thankful people has a way of uplifting a person. Lana and Scott's enthusiasm about life, regardless of the curveballs that had been thrown at them, was contagious.

    The next morning, George drove up the long dirt campground road to pick me up. "I want to take you to breakfast to meet some of the locals," he said. I said goodbye to Lana and Scott, got one last big kiss from Duke, and hopped into George's truck after heaving Wilson into its bed.

    This meeting of the locals took place at the local IGA grocery store, which sat across the street from Gone Bananas. Upon entering the door, we curved left and joined a few older guys at a round table in the center of a small dining area. George said, "This place has the best biscuits and gravy you'll ever have." I suspected that he was a bit biased, considering that his wife was the cook, but he was right. Once I sat down with my place and dug in, the truth revealed itself in the form of thick, country style white gravy with bits of ground sausage over fluffy biscuits. It was the exact sort of breakfast my weary muscles were begging for.

The locals George wanted me to meet were every bit as entertaining as I'd anticipated they would be, each in their own simple way. Their conversation topics switched between the weather, crops, the river, and who had died recently. When topics ran dry, they just began the process over again.

"I hope you get to meet Rex!" George said excitedly as I sipped a Coke while everyone else drank their coffees, "He's quite a character." Sure enough, the famed Rex eventually did make an appearance. Aided by a woman who appeared to be his daughter, Rex shuffled over to the table. His feet never left the ground as he did a slow ski across the linoleum floor and took a seat next to me. A cup of coffee was promptly delivered to him. He sat there sipping it, looking around at all the other faces around the table with a smile.

Rex was short and wearing faded overalls with a black t-shirt underneath them. His hands were big with broad fingers. They looked strong even after nearly a century of use. Rex was 97 years old. His voice was gentle, but commanded attention. Everyone listened when Rex had something to say. My favorite piece of information I picked up about his long life came when he said, "I've been married to my wife for 71 years and never been unfaithful once."

Rex was a Grayville legend who seemed almost as old as the town itself. He said he had lived in Grayville since before the river changed paths. I didn't exactly know what that meant, but it sounded like it had happened a long time ago.

~

I met up with Braden Willis, a newspaper reporter who wanted to interview me, in Carmi. After meeting in his downtown office, we went across the street to the VFW to have a couple of beers and do the interview. Braden walked me along the long wall of Carmi veterans from a wide range of wars and told me about many of them. He had been a Marine himself.

After the interview and several beers, Braden offered me an invitation to crash in the spare room at his apartment for the night, which I accepted. He also called his parents, who lived in Enfield, which was about 10 miles west of Carmi, to ask them if they would be willing to host me the following night. They said they would. I was happy to know where I would be staying a night in advance. That didn't happen often.

The next day, I walked to Enfield and met Braden's parents, Braden Sr. and Susie. Susie filled a frosted mug with Coke for me and we all sat around and learned about each other. Braden was a former Marine who had served in Vietnam, so I had a lot of questions for him, which he graciously answered. He had also been a police officer for many years and was currently a pastor. They were wonderful hosts for the night. I bid them goodbye the next morning to continue west. Little did I know, I'd soon be back.

~

McLeansboro was an easy 11 mile walk from Enfield. Braden and Susie had set me up in advance with a host family there. This was how things worked in the Midwest. One family would just pass me off to the next one down the line. My hosts after this most recent hiker hand-off were Gary and Kathy.

I went into the McDonald's in McLeansboro to wait for Gary and Kathy's son to come pick me up. He was a local police officer and would be driving me out to their farm outside of town in the afternoon. I sat down to eat, and a couple of old ladies came up and sat right next to me at my table. I was the only other person in the dining area and there were many empty tables, but they came over and sat with me to talk, I guess. We talked about all kinds of things and I said, "I heard Jerry Sloan is from McLeansboro. I'm a big fan of his. Do either of you know him?" Jerry Sloan is a basketball legend who saw great success in the NBA as both as a player and coach. The old ladies looked at each other and giggled. "You're having lunch with his sisters!" the oldest one said excitedly. So there I sat eating lunch with Jerry Sloan's sisters as they told me all about him.

I was soon picked up and on my way to Gary and Kathy's farm. Gary took me on a tour of the land he managed and owned. It was a huge plot of acreage that had to have spread across most of the county. We rode down long dirt roads in his truck. I saw an Amish family at work in a field. There were four or five kids ranging in age from toddlers to teenagers working away. The mother was weeding with one arm and cradling an infant in her other.

Gary went back to work right when we got back to the house, and I was told to go inside and relax. As I headed to the door, I saw Gary begin to collect various debris and brush to burn, and asked if he minded if I helped out. He looked surprised, but said it would be fine. We gathered all sorts of stuff into a pile and set it on fire. It felt satisfying to do some kind of manual labor other than walking.

Life On Foot

~

In the morning, menacing clouds rolled in from a couple different directions, but I was intent on moving westward anyway. I felt confident that I could make the 22 miles to Benton, regardless of whatever Mother Nature felt like throwing my way. It wasn't like I hadn't seen rain before. I just happened to be walking through the Midwest during the rainiest spring in 100 years, and had made it ok so far.

This proved to be a very bad idea. About 12 miles into this latest fool's errand I was thoroughly soaked. The temperature took a dive as soon as the rain began, and I was shivering. The clouds got progressively darker and poured massive raindrops consistently for hours. I ran into an unused barn just off the road and removed as many articles of my sopping wet clothing as I could, hoping they might dry out. I ate a bunch of food, drank water, and walked around briskly to try and warm up, but couldn't manage to do it inside the drafty barn. It kept me out of the rain but not the cold wind. I noticed that my hands were turning purple. I grabbed a small mirror and looked at my face, which was a ghostly shade of pale white.

Hitchhiking to Benton became my only real option. I put my clothes back on in the barn and prepared to walk back to the road. Putting on cold, damp clothes when you are already cold and damp is one of the most miserable things a person can do to themselves. I got back out to the road in the rain and stuck my thumb up, and the first car that approached stopped. I threw my stuff into the trunk of the small car, but just as I slammed it shut an SUV pulled up to my left, startling me. A hand reached out of the SUV window and there was a large McDonald's Coke presented to me.

It was Braden and Susie Willis. They had gotten worried about me after seeing the weather, and driven about 45 minutes to track me down. "Get on in," Susie said, "Come to the house for the weekend (it was Friday), go to church with us on Sunday, and you can start fresh on Monday."

I pulled Wilson out of the trunk of the car I had flagged down just seconds earlier and transferred it to Braden and Susie's vehicle. I apologized for wasting my would-be rescuers' time and hopped in with Braden and Susie for the ride back to Enfield. I sat in the back seat and drank the Coke, feeling amazed at my good fortune.

The entire Willis family spoiled me all weekend. Saturday was spent moving as little as possible and eating as much as I could. On Sunday I went to church and heard Braden deliver a sermon. Nearly everyone in the congregation came up to introduce themselves and wish me luck on my journey. After church I joined in on a Willis family Sunday lunch.

After my timely absorption into the Willis family, I resumed my walking once again out of Benton and enjoyed several days of fairly uneventful trekking. I passed through Chester, the official home of Popeye The Sailor Man, the famous cartoon character. Popeye's creator, Elzie Segar, grew up in Chester and based many of the characters in his cartoons on residents of the town.

Chester was the last place I saw in Illinois before crossing the Mississippi River into Missouri. There was a bronze statue of Popeye on the west side of town right by the Chester Bridge, my pathway into The Show-Me State. The bridge was illegal to cross on foot, so I hitched a ride across with an older couple I met at a gas station. I saw only a brief glimpse of the calm, fat river as we rushed over it. I got dropped off next to a corn field just over the river. It was the first time I had ever been west of the mighty Mississippi.

Chapter 12: Storms

I was surrounded by a pack of four vicious stray dogs just over the Missouri border. Two approached me from the front, two from behind. They were hunting. They surrounded me and snarled and barked. I swung my walking stick while spinning around in a circle to keep them all at bay. They snapped their teeth at the stick and stayed just outside its striking range in between short charges toward me. My goal while doing this was simply to make killing me more trouble than it would be worth for the dogs. It ended up working, and they eventually withdrew. The dogs retreated into the same tall grass they had so stealthily materialized out of just a few minutes earlier. They looked skinny and hungry as they slinked away with their heads down low. I hoped an easier meal was waiting for them out there somewhere.

The landscape mimicked what I had already grown accustomed to in Illinois. The hills rolled and rolled and rolled. I rescued a lot of turtles from being run over by cars as they attempted to slowly cross the road. There was a lot of road kill in eastern Missouri, mostly armadillos and deer. The sweltering summer heat caused the decomposing armadillos to begin cooking on the sizzling pavement. The resulting smell made me gag for miles on end. Dead deer were everywhere along the road, several per mile through some areas.

I spent a lot of time prying ticks off my body and clothing, usually at the rate of about 20-30 a day. That rate would continue all the way through mid-Kansas. Bugs swarmed my tent with a vengeance every night. Each morning I brushed handfuls of ticks, beetles, slugs, moths, and whatever other creepy crawlies roamed the forest floor at night off its sides and bottom. One night,

I awoke to a distinct tickling sensation on my chest. I turned on my headlamp and looked down while hoping that I was just imagining things. I was not. There were four very real ticks making their way up my chest toward my face. I had already picked about a dozen of them off myself before crawling into my tent. They were absolutely everywhere.

It rained a lot during these days, and I kept hearing warnings about oncoming storms that had the potential to be severe. It was tornado season.

On May 22, I stopped at a convenience store in the middle of nowhere. I drank 44 ounces of Mountain Dew, talked with some local folks, and then walked up the road to find a place to camp. The spot I chose was about 100 yards off the road and completely secluded. Not a soul in the world knew where I was. I spent the afternoon reading and fell asleep early in the evening.

And then the storm came. Being completely out of contact with the world, I had no idea about the devastation that had taken place just hours earlier in Joplin, Missouri, some 250 miles west of my location.

I awoke suddenly during the night. It sounded like a freight train was bearing down on me at full throttle. Rain slammed against my tent and the ground that surrounded it so fiercely that drops splashed up from underneath my rain fly and soaked my sleeping bag. The wind howled through the trees and nearly blew my tent flat, even though I was in a densely forested area protected from most of its force. Lightning bolts cracked in such close succession that the entire forest was brightly illuminated for several seconds at a time. Branches snapped and fell to the ground all around me, some smaller ones actually making contact with my tent. I laid flat and covered my head with my arms. I am not sure how long it all lasted.

When I emerged from my tent in the morning, my surroundings were entirely different from when I had gone into it the previous evening. There were downed branches all over the place, and every inch of the forest was disturbed in some way. I knew it had been a severe storm, but didn't yet realize that 250 miles west of me, 158 people were dead and 1,000 were injured as a result of the same mass of treacherous weather. I had been hit by the remnants of the same weather system that had virtually demolished Joplin. I was fortunate that it had lost a bit of steam by the time it landed on my head.

I turned on my phone and it exploded with activity. There were at least a dozen text messages and voicemails waiting for me, and I immediately knew that something had gone very wrong. The messages said "Are you ok?" and "Call me ASAP!"

After scrambling over and under blown down trees and returning to the road, I found some phone signal and called my parents. My mom filled me in on what had happened first. It put a somber note on the day and marked the beginning of what would be a tough stretch of the walk mentally.

~

A couple of days after the storm, it was warm and birds were singing. A gentle breeze kept the temperature at a consistently pleasant level. Enjoying the weather completely, I took Wilson off to have a few minutes of rest on the side of the road.

Just as Wilson hit the ground I saw a small dog, maybe weighing about 30 pounds, running my direction across a yard on the other side of the road. He was barking, but in a friendly way, and seemed like he just wanted to say hello. I expected him to stop at the edge of the lawn like most dogs do when they live next to a busy road. They were typically pretty aware of traffic, especially in the Midwest where almost nobody used leashes or runs.

As I watched the silly dog I noticed a flash of red coming from my right. It was a car. At that same moment I also realized that the little dog was not stopping. He was dead set on coming over to say hi.

I tried to get the attention of the driver, but it was too late. The timing was perfectly awful. There was a sudden thud followed by a sickening crunch. My skin crawled as I heard the sounds. I screamed, "Fuck!" and scrambled to my feet. Running across the road, I saw the dog flopping around on the pavement. There was blood everywhere. I glanced up and there were two men, I assumed one of them to be the owner of the dog, standing on the porch of the mobile home the dog had run from. They saw the whole thing happen, yet didn't bother to move a muscle. They were more focused on finishing their cigarettes, I think. Real classy guys. Since they weren't going to do anything, I hurriedly picked the dog up and carried him off to the side of the road. He was still flopping around and it was hard to hold onto him, but I did.

I knelt down and held the dog in my arms while trying to soothe him. I ran my fingers gently across his head. His short, light brown fur was wet with blood. He looked right into my eyes as the last bit of life left him.

The idiots on the porch finally came over and asked if the dog was dead. I nodded yes. The lady who was driving the car that hit the dog came back. She didn't seem to care much about what had just happened either. It only took a minute before her and the two guys were cracking jokes and laughing. The owner of the dog said, "I don't give a damn about the dog, I just hope your car is okay," to the lady. My blood boiled when he said this, but I was just too sad to really do anything about it.

    I silently went back over to Wilson and tried to drink some water. My hands were shaking so much that I ended up pouring most of it down the front of my shirt and shorts. Tears ran down my sunbaked face. Looking at my hands and arms, I noticed the blood that was smeared all over them. I put some water into my hand and tried to wash it off, but it didn't work very well. It just spread it around more, if anything.

~

    Nearing Ironton that same day, a car pulled over ahead of me. The lady driving it knew who I was from a local newspaper and invited me to camp at her home, which was a short drive away. At that point I was ready to end the day no matter how far it was. I told her what had happened with the dog, which was a terrible idea, as I nearly broke down in front of her.

    Her name was Teri. She lived in a house with her mother, Bobbi, and her two children, Shayna and Vinny. Bobbi was upbeat, chain smoked Decade Reds, and looked just so damn happy to be alive. Teri was the same, minus the endless cigarettes. The whole family went out of their way to make me feel at home. Teri cooked dinner while I played basketball in the street with Vinny and Shayna. On what was one of the lowest morale days of the whole walk, spending time with such a caring family made everything bearable.

    That night, as I got into my tent and sat down on my sleeping bag, I heard a crack. I knew what had happened instantly. I had sat on my Kindle reader, my only source of entertainment after a long day of walking. The screen was shattered and it was no longer usable. It really wasn't my day.

~

The next morning, I began walking early as usual, but decided to call it a day not long after. The sky was turning into a mass of ghoulish, deep green and black clouds. I found the closest motel and checked in, figuring it was better to be safe than sorry, especially after what had happened in Joplin not long before. The weather held off for a while, but eventually did start getting ugly.

The tornado warning siren in town began to blare. The temperature dropped what had to have been 15 or 20 degrees in a matter of minutes. Hailstones in sizes ranging from dimes to quarters started pelting the roof of the hotel. It was hail like I had never seen before — a melee of ice just outside my motel room door.

The motel manager went room to room and told people to get into their bathtubs if things got much worse. As a kid from New England, I was thinking, *Well, this is it. This is how I die.* The whole tornado thing was brand new to me. Just days after hearing about Joplin and enduring that storm in my tent, my heart was pounding.

Vinny, Teri's son, sent me a text message that said, "What's up?"

I replied, "Freaking out a bit because of the weather! What are you doing?"

"Under a desk," he wrote back.

"Because of the weather?" I asked.

"Yeah," he replied calmly. It wasn't a big deal to Vinny at all.

After what seemed like hours, the siren of death stopped whining and the sky slowly cleared. I took a walk around the motel parking lot. Hailstones cracked under my boots. Several funnel clouds had formed, but none managed to build up enough steam to make contact with the ground. I was thankful that my tub would only be needed for bathing, not for hiding from murderous cyclones.

As my nerves slowly died down in my motel room, I got online and ordered Wilson II. Wilson II was a Schwinn Spirit Bike Trailer and would be replacing Wilson I. With handlebar and front wheel attachments, which turned the bike trailer into something more like a baby jogger, the new Wilson would be the perfect way for me to transition from carrying my gear, food, and water to pushing it. The weight of 45 pounds on my back at all times was destroying my knees and feet. This was a necessary move if I ever wanted to make it to San Francisco. It is rare for a cross-country walker to complete their entire trek with just a backpack. Once the Midwest starts to become the West, towns get considerably further apart, meaning a hiker has to carry much more food and water than normal to stay alive. Putting all that extra stuff in a cart you can push is much easier than toting it around on your back.

I also got in touch with Alana that day. I had heard from her now and then, but for the most part it seemed like she had no interest in what I was up to. It ate away at me more each day. She seemed to have moved on, which she should have. The unfortunate part about it was that I still loved her and missed her. I had gotten better at controlling such feelings, but what I was doing was still a selfish act in my mind. I didn't feel angry or frustrated with Alana at all, those feelings were all toward myself.

I was desperate to calm the storm going on in my head about all this, and came across that way to her. Desperation is rarely flattering. I said some things I shouldn't have and told her that I wished she would wait for me to get home so we could be together again. I don't know why I expected this to work, because it certainly hadn't when I'd tried it before back in Maryland.

Of course, this nonsense made her upset. She said there was no chance of us working things out. The phone line went silent, and that was it. After building up some solid momentum through Indiana and Illinois, I felt myself screeching to a halt. Things just seemed to keep going wrong, one right after the other. I guess that when it rains, it pours. Or hails.

~

I soon made it to the town of Licking, where I holed up in a hotel and prepared to take my only vacation from the walk, which was something I needed badly. Two friends of mine, Joel and Justin Runyon, were on the way to pick me up. We were going to take a road trip out to the World Domination Summit in Portland, Oregon, which is a yearly gathering for people who do unconventional things and want to meet, learn, and party with other people who do the same. I spent the next two weeks traveling around the West and having what was probably too good of a time in Portland. Joel and Justin dropped me back off in Licking, where I resumed walking with fresh legs and a cleared mind, this time with Wilson II. The difference between Wilson I and Wilson II was astounding. I floated 25 miles a day without being fatigued at all. I wished I had gotten rid of the backpack even sooner.

I did my first bridge camping in central Missouri. Camping underneath a bridge during nice weather is enjoyable. It's shaded and hidden. The first night was quiet, minus the occasional car driving overhead.

Camping underneath a bridge during bad weather, however, is a whole other beast, and the second night went differently. Logically, it seems like it would be a great idea to hide under a bridge to get out of the rain and wind, which it is. The problem with this is that every creature and insect within several miles of the bridge you're under thinks it's a great idea as well.

Bugs of every type made the trip under the bridge as the rain began coming down. Dueling swarms competed for the limited air space. The air under the bridge was hot and stagnant. My legs were sliced from the prickly bushes that I had to walk through to get underneath the bridge. Sweat poured into my wounds and stung constantly. I was tent bound. I couldn't leave or I would be overtaken by the insect insurrection.

Like many things in life, it was all agonizing for a while until it suddenly became beautiful. Fireflies became the dominant swarm. They were everywhere, just thousands of swirling, illuminated dots. There was hardly an inch of space underneath the bridge that wasn't occupied by their gentle glow. Seeing such beauty calmed me down. The stinging in my legs subsided and I drifted off to sleep.

Aside from being awoken in the middle of the night by the sounds of a small animal being savagely murdered by a fox just a few feet from my tent, things went smoothly under the bridge. It was difficult to fall back asleep after hearing the cries of the little beast being slaughtered and the sounds of ripping flesh and chewing, but I managed to do it.

~

My last night in Missouri was spent attempting to sleep in a shed next to a church. The operators of this church did not know I was inside their shed. The shed was a basic one, made of nothing but low-quality wooden beams and sheets of metal roofing. A storm rolled in, bringing wind that blew rain through the shed door and directly into my tent. I scrambled to attach my tent's rainfly in the dark. A section of the shed's metal roofing was loose, so each gust of wind picked it up and slammed it down against the wooden beams. This went on all night without interruption. BANG, BANG, BANG. I finally gave up on sleeping at around 5 AM and packed up my things, doubting that I could make it to the nearby Kansas line without collapsing. I had gotten perhaps an hour of sleep.

My phone buzzed as I groggily turned it on. A new friend I'd met recently had sent me a text message over the course of the night, and I perked up a little after seeing it. The strangest things would often keep me moving forward, even in tough circumstances. Sometimes it was the adrenaline rush that came from almost being hit by a car, others it was a friendly wave from a motorist or finding something funny on the side of the road, such as a Kenny Rogers CD or a bra.

I walked out onto yet another stretch of highway in the foggy, sleepy dawn. It was a simple message from a pretty girl that got me all the way to Kansas from there.

Chapter 13: Can I See The Baby?

Everybody told me not to walk across Kansas. It was typical for people I met to warn me about the next state in line, as there are often negative stereotypes and rivalries between neighboring states, but *everybody* warned me about Kansas. From Delaware through Missouri, people said I was crazy to *want* to walk across it. From Colorado to California, they told me I was crazy because I actually *did*. When I got back to Maine after the walk, people asked, "What did you do about Kansas?" They said it was too boring to walk across, that its residents were strange and unwelcoming, that small town Kansas police would run me out of town. These people all turned out to be full of crap. Kansas would end up being one of my favorite states of the walk.

I passed through Bronson, a miniscule town of about 320 people, during my first day in the state. A sign on the outskirts of town read: Bronson, Kansas - Home Of The First World Championship Horseshoe Pitch - 1909. It marked the beginning of what seemed to be a constant battle between towns to one-up each other, no matter how odd their town slogans or claims to fame were. Even the most obscure facts and far-fetched claims were grasped onto by locals searching for some sort of notoriety and reputation for their homes.

The landscape opened up and became flat. Very flat. But in other areas it would be hilly, then flat again. Fields of wheat, soybeans, and corn were the standard. Farmers worked away and waved at me from their tractors.

In Iola, I wandered into a McDonald's in search of some free WiFi, a cold drink, and possibly some satisfying local conversation. I would get all three. Almost immediately after walking in the door I was greeted with a question that caught me off guard from an older gentleman sitting at a nearby table. He wore a perfectly white tee shirt under baggy overalls.

"Where are *yeeeouuu* from?" he belted out.

"I'm from Maine."

Nothing but a blank stare from the old man.

I repeated myself.

More blank staring.

"The state that's way up in the northeastern corner of the country," I said, then he understood.

I sat down one table over from the old fellow and explained to him that I was just traveling through town on the way to somewhere else. We talked about a selection of random things and both commented on the hot weather. He had a fly swatter sitting on the table next to his hand. His small cup of coffee was placed neatly on a napkin.

I watched him swat at flies for a while and asked him every now and then, "Did you get it?"

"Nope, don't think so," he would say.

A preacher walked in and knew the old man. We were introduced and talked for a few minutes. Before he left he gave me $20.00.

I said, "You don't need to do that."

"I know, but he does," he said as he pointed to the sky.

~

It was a sweltering day when I arrived in Yates Center a day later. I longed for any sort of cold liquid dispensing store or machine to appear through the waves of heat rising off the pavement ahead. A sign along the road read: Welcome To Yates Center - Hay Capital Of The World. It seemed like a big claim for a town of about 1,400 people. I stumbled to the closest store on the edge of town on the brink of heat exhaustion and promptly downed two drinks.

Drinks downed, I headed south out of town to look for a campground the local police dispatch had informed me of. I noticed an old man wandering toward me across his lawn as I struggled along. He was wearing a crisp, blue button up shirt, jeans, and a trucker-style hat. The hat was not achieving a snug fit, just resting lazily on top of his partially bald head. His house was not fancy by any means, but showed the signs of a having a prideful owner. Everything on the property was in order and clean, and the grass had just been cut. I noticed a black Ford Model T in the garage.

"Hey there, can I see the baby?" he asked.

"Sorry, no baby," I replied with a laugh, "Just my camping gear. I'm walking across the country and use this stroller to push my stuff around."

The old man talked softly and slowly and his laugh was the same. "Huh... Huh... Huuuh..."

"My name's Bishop," he said, "Joshua Bishop."

As with most Kansas folks, all it took was a short introduction and I was in for a long conversation with Joshua. It was just fine with me. He possessed a wealth of local knowledge and had lived in Yates Center almost his whole life. He had more kids and grandkids than I even thought was humanly possible. "I just love being around my grandkids," he said with a grandfatherly smile as he told me about each of them.

Joshua looked to be about 70 years old. When he told me he was actually 83, I said, "You've got to be the youngest looking 83 year old I've ever seen. What's the secret?"

"Never had a drink in my life and never smoked," he said proudly. So that settled that.

I parted ways with Mr. Bishop after talking on his lawn for a while and made my way to the local campground. There was only a single small RV there, so I took my time choosing the perfect place to call home for the night. It was a fairly nice place with electricity hookups and clean water, which I sat down and drank a half-gallon of before doing anything else.

The bathrooms were in awful shape. They were narrow concrete buildings with no doors. There were no doors on the bathroom stalls either. I guess you take what you can get at a free campground. What I had thought to be the greatest part about the place turned out to actually be the worst. Even worse than the no-door bathrooms. There was a crystal clear lake about a hundred yards away. It's cool waters called to me. Eagerly approaching it and expecting to be just seconds away from hurling myself in, I was greeted with a sign. Signs were always ruining things for me — no camping, no loitering, next service 73 miles, store closed. In this case, the sign read: NO SWIMMING ALLOWED.

It turned out that this body of water, my savior in the unforgiving heat, was a reservoir for the local water supply. I watched as a boat with an electric motor skimmed across it. Boating was allowed, swimming was not. I sat next to the reservoir for a while and contemplated just jumping in anyway, but chose not to. I ran the water from the pump at my campsite over my head for a minute, which helped. I cooked dinner and enjoyed the cooler evening temperatures. The sky glowed orange. Kansas sunsets were the best I'd come across yet.

~

Life On Foot 141

The next morning, a Ford Taurus came noisily down the dirt campground road and stopped by my campsite as I was packing up. It was Mr. Bishop. "Wanted to bring you a few dollars so you can get yourself a nice breakfast at the diner in town. And here's an envelope with my address on it. Send me a note when you make it to California," he said.

I thanked him, said that it was a pleasure to have met him, and that I would not only send a letter, but call him too when I hit the ocean.

Mr. Bishop recommended The Tip Top Cafe for breakfast, which sat about a mile away. I made the short walk there after getting Wilson packed up. I parked Wilson and walked in as a few of the locals inside looked at me curiously. I smiled and nodded. They smiled and nodded back.

Eating at the Tip Top Cafe was like eating at home. It was comfortable and friendly. Kansas University memorabilia lined each of its walls. There were KU posters, clocks, calendars, and stuffed animals to be seen. There were a few booth tables and a bar style counter, where a few men sat sipping coffee and talking about the wheat harvest. Their muddy boots left little spots of dirt on the floor. Every conversation I eavesdropped on had to do with either the crops or the weather.

The dining room was small, but didn't feel cramped. There were windows letting in the morning sunlight and the walls were clean and white. If you looked at the proper angle from many of the tables, you could see into the kitchen. Glasses were stacked neatly behind the counter next to a pile of silverware wrapped in paper napkins and a couple of old coffee machines.

A man walked in and sat alone at the table adjacent to me. He had "regular" written all over him. The man removed his tattered hat and sat patiently with his hands folded in front of him as if he was praying. His jeans and shirt were dusty. He was the type of guy who got a half-day's work done before most folks even woke up in the morning. A full breakfast magically appeared in front of him within a few minutes. He hadn't uttered a word since he had walked in, except for when he greeted the waitress with a nod and a "Mornin'."

A busy lady in the kitchen, who appeared to be doing all of the cooking on her own, kept poking her head out into the dining area. She surveyed the room every once in a while, then darted back to her duties through the open door. Through that same door I could hear the faint crackling of bacon and sausage being cooked.

My waitress took my order for an omelet and jotted it down on a small pad of paper, then tucked it back into her apron pocket. The food came quickly. I ate quietly and watched as the rugged farmers took their last sips of coffee, said goodbye to their buddies, and hit the parking lot to start their dirt covered, rusty trucks. *Until tomorrow, boys*, I thought. They were off to do something that would add more dirt and rust to their trucks, I assumed.

I looked out the window. Traffic trickled slowly down West Mary Street. The easy pace of Yates Center had drawn me right in. That table could have easily remained my perch for the rest of the day. I thought to myself about how most people try to *experience* America. They race between the National Parks and the landmarks they are supposed to see on busy, soul sucking Interstate highways. The journey becomes a well-calculated plan of exits and efficiency. I thought of how much I cherished the glimpse into America that was the small town diner with regular people as regulars, complete with muddy boots and cheap coffee, rusty trucks, and dull conversations about the weather.

Chapter 14: Midway U.S.A.

Soon after leaving Yates Center I entered the Flint Hills region of Kansas. The Flint Hills are home to the most pristine prairie land on the continent. The vast majority of the land has never been touched with a plow or agricultural tool of any kind. Kansas' reputation for flat, monotonous stretches of land has no validity there. Hills varying in size between barely noticeable bumps and steady mile long inclines that would make anybody break a sweat spread out in every direction. These natural undulations were coated in grasses such as Indian grass, bluestem, and switchgrass. All of my senses were open to their maximum capacities. Each hill seemed different in a myriad of ways. I could see the wind coming, the prairie grasses bending in my direction from its invisible push. The weather was perfect. The skinny forests between the open patches of prairie were teeming with life.

In the coming days I passed though Eureka, El Dorado, Whitewater (Whitewater, Kansas - A Little Town With A Big Heart) and Burrton. Outside of Burrton I camped at an RV park and made fast friends with a crew of four nomadic construction workers named Jim, Jim, Chuck, and Gary. They moved constantly to find work and lived at campgrounds as they migrated about.

We drank several beers together and I enjoyed listening to their crude construction worker talk. Chuck was a magnificent redneck. He puffed out his bare, hairy chest as he spoke and swore like a pirate. He was wearing jeans that had to have been at least 10 years old and solid steel-toe work boots. He had a mullet-esque haircut and a mustache so thick that it looked like a squirrel had been glued below his nose.

    Appearances aside, Chuck also showcased a certain level of ingenuity that the redneck subculture is well known for. For example, Chuck lived in an unnecessarily large family sized tent by himself. He had cut an opening into one of the tent's walls, into which he installed an air conditioner. The air conditioner was supported by an awkwardly shaped structure made of 2 x 4 boards and hooked up to a hole cut out of the tent's wall with a duct-tape seal. It did not look great by any means, but it was functional. Functional enough to be the envy of everyone else at the campground. When he decided to call it a night and crawled into his gigantic tent, Chuck zipped the door shut and yelled, "It's fuckin' chilly in here!" Everyone around scoffed and told him to fuck off. Nobody else would be experiencing the level of luxury that Chuck had achieved for himself. We all drank our beers a little bit faster after Chuck retired for the night. He had reminded us of what was ahead. The sticky air was coming for each of us in due time. So we drank. If you can't be comfortable, you might as well be drunk.

    In Stafford, I ran into one of the many crazies I often encountered on the road. I was setting up my camp at the town park when he approached me to say hello. Our conversation went well at first. He asked me how people were treating me during my travels. I said, "They have been amazing, I've found that most people are really good."

    "No they're not!" he shouted, "We are born evil and full of sin and without hope for changin' it!"

    "I'm afraid I have to disagree with you there," I said kindly.

    "We are born in sin! Just look at the Bible!"

    "Yeah."

"God's gonna destroy this all soon because of the sin, ya know? And I'll tell ya how he's gonna do it."
I couldn't help myself. "How's that?"
"The Germans. The damn Germans have been slowly building up strength and we haven't even noticed. We've been so focused on China! I'm tellin' ya, soon the Germans are gonna nuke us and whoever is left will be speakin' German! Not Chinese! German!"
"So God is going to use the Germans to destroy us because of our sin? Just want to make sure I have it right."
"I know what you're doin'! You think I'm full of it! But someday, when it all happens, you're gonna remember me and what I said to ya here today!" he yelled. The man then walked away while continuing to rant on to himself until I couldn't hear him anymore, which was nice.
I celebrated the Fourth of July in Macksville. And by celebrated I mean that I jumped around in a sprinkler in the town park like a child, read a book, and went to bed around 8 PM. The town park, where my tent was set up, was empty and noiseless until the fireworks started. They sounded off from every corner of town after the sun disappeared for the day. A couple of attractive young women who were about my age approached my tent as I laid inside it in a sweaty heap. I could not have looked more unattractive. They gave me a warm can of beer and wished me a happy Fourth. I tried to thank them, but tripped over my words and ended up sounding more foolish than appreciative. I must have forgotten how to talk to girls somewhere along the way. It had been a long walk.

~

The Kansas sun was scorching my skin and spirit as the temperature hit 105 degrees. A semi truck roared down the road in my direction. I shifted from my safe position on the far left side of the shoulder toward the road just slightly. I wanted to get as close to the path of the truck as I could manage without being hit by it. I knew the breeze it would create in passing me would give me a brief, blissful flash of relief from the heat. I inched closer and closer toward the road as the truck blew by me. The thundering burst of wind that followed it blew my straw hat clear off my head and back into a roadside ditch. I walked back to pick it up and hoped another truck would be along soon. The road was clear in both directions after I got my hat back on. I stepped off the shoulder and onto the smooth pavement. Something felt different after a minute or two. The rubber soles of my boots were melting and sticking to the road, so I went back to the cooler gravel shoulder.

The end of my 25 mile day was going to be the small town of Kinsley. I wouldn't take a single step further. A couple of close calls with errant drivers and the searing heat had driven me to the end of my wits. Through the waves of superheated air rising from the road I saw salvation in the form of a gas station. It was a hideous concrete block building, but at that moment it was the most beautiful place in the world. I parked Wilson and looked forward to the glorious moment when the air conditioning would envelop me. The door opened and in I went. It was cool, but not as cool as I thought it would be. I went to the nearest drink cooler, opened its door, and put my head inside it. Much better. Once I no longer felt like I was on fire, I grabbed two large drinks and made my way to the store's checkout counter.

"Is it you that's walkin' down the highway?" asked the cashier.

Life On Foot

"Yup, that's me. It's a hot one out there," I said, mustering every last bit of enthusiasm I had, which wasn't much.

"I've been waitin' for ya, saw ya walkin' earlier this mornin' on my way to work," she said with a smile, "Ya want somethin' to eat?"

"I always want something to eat."

"Let me make ya our beef enchilada lunch. Go out back and sit in the break room and relax. There's a nice fan blowin' back there. I'll bring it back to ya," she said, then turned around to get started on my meal.

"You just made my entire day," I said before stumbling back to the closet-like break room.

A few minutes later, she appeared with a take-out box, handed it over, and told me to relax and hang out for as long as I wanted to. The box was monstrous. It had to have weighed at least two pounds. A swirling cloud of steam prevented me from seeing what was inside it for a moment after I lifted its lid. Two hefty enchiladas and a pile of tortilla chips came into view once the steam cleared. Everything in the box was covered in that suspicious and delicious goopy yellow nacho cheese that gas stations have.

About half of the enchilada mountain was down by the time I gave in and could eat no more. I practically rolled out of the chair, thanked the lady at the counter several times, then made my way toward the door. "Hold on a sec! Here are a couple boxes of donuts and pastries we had left from this mornin', they're all yours," she said from behind the counter as she handed me two boxes containing about a dozen donuts and pastries. Thanking her once more, I stepped back out into the Kansas oven.

There was a milk delivery truck parked next to Wilson when I went outside. The driver was leaning against its back bumper and looked like he was in search of some conversation. We talked for a few minutes and he went on and on about the wonders of Kansas. He said, "John Wayne himself said there's nothing like a Kansas sunset. When I heard him say that on the radio one time, I just about cried."

With a lead on a place to camp a mile ahead, I trudged away from the store. It would be a slow mile. I was beyond weary and felt anchored down by the enchiladas and mystery cheese. At the first intersection past the gas station, a truck pulled up and stopped to let me cross the street. Looking out the rolled down driver's side window of the beat up Ford F-150 was a young kid. He couldn't have been more than ten or eleven years old at the most. I gave him a curious look. *Seriously, kid*? He looked at me, nodded his head with a mischievous smirk on his face, then hit the gas. I'm not sure how he was even able to reach the pedal. The truck's wheels spun in the loose gravel on the road before suddenly finding their grip. The truck lurched forward, then crossed the street and disappeared. Welcome to Kansas.

Arriving at a rest area at the intersection of U.S. Highways 50 and 56 on the west side of town, I was delighted to see a bathroom, outdoor water pump, and covered picnic area. There was also an old steam locomotive there, which sat parked on a short strip of abandoned railroad track. The locomotive was a remnant of the old Atchison, Topeka and Santa Fe Railway. The Edwards County Museum, an old church building, and a fenced in area with various pieces of antique farm equipment on display also took up small areas of the park. Despite these attractions, there was something else that had my attention. It was a sign. This sign featured two prominent white arrows that

Life On Foot 151

pointed in opposite directions — one to the east, one to the west. The eastward pointing arrow read: NEW YORK 1561 MI. The westward one read: SAN FRANCISCO 1561 MI. According to the sign between the arrows, I was at Midway U.S.A., half way between New York and San Francisco. I let out a loud yell in celebration. I got goosebumps and smiled so big it made my cheeks hurt. San Francisco. Apparently it actually did exist.

Chapter 15: Coke Machine Blues

The sign that welcomed me to Dodge City was topped by a gang of metal silhouette horsemen. They could have been a harmless group of cowboys herding livestock, or maybe even a posse of desperadoes running from the law. Either way, they provided a fitting initial greeting to one of America's most notorious Wild West towns.

Dodge City grew up out of Fort Dodge, a post Civil War outpost along the Santa Fe Trail. From its humble beginnings, it didn't take long for Dodge City to become a vital commercial hub as America rapidly expanded westward. The buffalo hunting and cattle trades boomed in the area, bringing with them a rowdy gang of characters including cowboys, buffalo hunters, gamblers, and outlaws, all of whom had a passion for Dodge City's plentiful whisky, gambling, and women. Dodge City was the place where these rugged people of the West could go to spend their hard earned wages on all their favorite vices and the tools necessary for their trades.

I got into town in the early afternoon and made my way to the Boot Hill Museum, a place in Dodge City that had been recommended to me many times. The small admission fee to the museum proved to be well worth the expense. I proceeded out onto Front Street, the historic main vein of commerce of old Dodge City that had been carefully restored to look nearly exactly as it did in 1876. As I walked along Front Street, I stepped back into my favorite era of American history. The buildings along the Front Street boardwalk had tall false fronts and wooden awnings that provided shade from the midday sun. I walked through a group of four re-enactors who were sitting on a bench. The cowboys said "Howdy" and tipped their hats as I made my way by. I passed the famous Long Branch Saloon, where numerous fabled shootouts and violent fights had taken place during Dodge's wilder days. Just to give you an idea of the level of violence during these times, according to many sources, around 30 murders took place there in the few years around 1872, the year Dodge City was officially established — an astounding figure for a town with a population of only around 500 people.

Nearby was a replication of the Union Church, where legendary law officers of Dodge City, Bat Masterson and Wyatt Earp, were deacons. The church struggled to bring some reform to what was known at the time as "The Wickedest Little City In America." In 1878, after several decades of virtually uninterrupted debauchery, the local newspaper in Dodge City wrote in regard to the church being built: "The wicked city of Dodge can at last boast of a Christian organization."

The most interesting and entertaining aspect of the Boot Hill Museum was Boot Hill itself, the old local cemetery. Called Boot Hill because the poor souls laid to rest there were often buried hastily with their boots still on, the cemetery gave a clear impression of how rough the initial years of Dodge City's existence were. While some of the bodies that had been buried there had been moved over the years, many still remained in their original locations in a compact, fully intact corner of the old hill.

The epitaphs written by the inhabitants of Dodge City were blunt, depressing, and more often than not, hilarious. There were carefully researched epitaphs on most of the wooden grave markers, as well as signs giving details about the ways in which many Boot Hill occupants had passed.

One of my favorite epitaphs was for an unfortunate bugger named Edward Hurley, who was shot and killed on January 17, 1873. It read: "He drank too much and loved unwisely." Another was for a bold man named George Hoyt, which read: "One night he took a pot shot at Wyatt Earp." A man named McDermott was "plugged" and buried at Boot Hill. Barney Cullen was killed during a shooting spree in a saloon. Alice Chambers, a Dodge City prostitute, was the only woman ever buried at Boot Hill. Her last words were recorded as being, "Circumstances led me to this end."

After taking in everything I could, I enjoyed one last walk down the Front Street boardwalk. The same posse of re-enactors I'd seen earlier walked toward me, their boots knocking loudly on the faded boards. A hot prairie breeze hit my face. Although the city had much more to offer than I had gotten to see, it was nearing dark and my lack of an overnight connection forced me to think about leaving. Overall, Dodge City was exactly what I'd hoped it would be. I learned about the history of the place while there, and was able to gain an even stronger appreciation than I already had for the tough and determined people who settled the American West.

As I was walking along the west side of Dodge City on Highway 50 and evaluating my camping options, a large cattle truck barreled toward me. Hundreds of them did on a daily basis, so I didn't think anything of it at first. As it got closer, however, I looked up just at the right moment to see a wide stream of cow urine flying in my direction. The sides of the cattle trailer were slotted, meaning a rear-facing cow could do their business out the side of it.

I jumped to my left while pushing Wilson into the ditch as the stream of rancid liquid missed me by about two feet, landing with a splash on the asphalt just behind me. It was a sign if I'd ever seen one. It was time to get the hell out of Dodge.

~

Had the cow piss actually hit me, I wouldn't have been in as bad of a situation as you might think. This is because a roadside traveler always has a bathing option in large scale farmland, which comes in the form of irrigation equipment. Such equipment can be the perfect solution for a quick wash or cool off session. In fields as expansive as the ones in Kansas, most farmers use pivoting or laterally moving sprayers. These giant pieces of equipment are hundreds of feet long and move automatically on wheels. Their movements are controlled by the specifications programmed into the sprayer's built-in timers. As a result, entire fields can be watered without even the smallest bit of human effort. As far as I could tell, a company called Reinke had a complete monopoly on the making and selling of them. I always just called them Reinkes.

Most of the fields the Reinkes were in had signs warning that they were not to be trespassed on, but I had long since stopped following such suggestions. I'd look both ways down the road, scan the field for any trucks or tractors, then bound toward the cool waters. Seconds later I would feel refreshed and renewed, then walk back to the road soaking wet and continue along my way.

In the same way that Reinkes were a welcomed break from the Kansas temperatures, road signs served as much needed sources of motivation while trudging down straight and flat highways that felt as if they would go on forever. Even small signs were visible from faraway distances because of the level layout of the

Life On Foot

land. Who knew what type of information an upcoming sign would hold? A historical marker or a mileage figure to the next town, perhaps? Maybe a hint about a place where I could get myself a cold drink? Oftentimes, however, this excitement was unwarranted. Too often I overexerted myself just to read a stupid sign. I'd bust ass down roads that felt like stovetops to read something like: Stoneberger Crested Wheatgrass Seeding - Seeded 1958.

With this being said, I did come across a sign west of Dodge City that deserved the anticipation I felt for it. I approached the sign during the steadily dimming last hour of daylight. It read: Santa Fe Trail Ruts. Santa Fe Trail stuff was all around, but it was the first time I had heard of wagon ruts still being visible. I walked off the road and into the prairie, and soon found the ruts that had been left by the wagons of travelers long since gone.

I have always been a bit of a time traveler when visiting historic places, which makes me an annoying person to visit them with. My mind wanders to distant times in vivid daydreams and I essentially disappear. I planted my feet firmly in the coarse grass under me and began thinking. I went back to the 1820s. A train of wagons found its way across the same open prairie I was standing in. I saw its members stop and admire the same orange Kansas sunset I was watching at that moment in real time. It was so bright and full of promise that it brought tears to their eyes. These travelers continued west and were followed by others. The passing of the years sped up and the wagons stopped. A train whistle blared just out of sight. Motorized tractors appeared on the prairie and harvested waves of wheat. An asphalt highway came together. Fences were built, cattle were raised. The wagon wheel ruts became less noticeable, but could still be seen if I looked hard enough. Tourists flocked from all over. I saw myself marching down the highway.

A whipping surge of wind snapped me back to the real world. It was a bizarrely lucid daydream. I'm not really sure how long it lasted. All I know is that I went somewhere else for a while and that it was nice. I noticed myself growing more out of touch with reality by the mile. It was a sensation that I decided to explore instead of avoid. I knew if there was ever a time to embrace the crazy, this was it.

Thinking about my newfound kookiness and how delightful I was finding it to be, I began my normal back to the road routine — check for wallet, phone, camera, a little bend forward to stretch my calves. My legs then instinctively started to propel me toward the setting sun. It was a familiar sensation facing into the orange glow, feeling the warm prairie air on my face, and listening to the whooshing of billions of stalks of wheat being tossed around by the wind, which seemed to come from every direction at once. It was a typical evening on the roadside in many ways, but something did feel different. I felt like I was less alone. Like I was traveling with untold thousands of fellow dreamers.

~

That night I walked from 6 PM until 1 AM. It was my first night hiking experience. I ambled down the road under faint moonlight. Lightning ignited on the horizon fifty miles away. A train rumbled down the tracks that ran alongside the road, and its conductor waved at me. A cop stopped to check on me and wished me luck the rest of the way. The particular stretch of road I was on was no more dangerous than it would have been during the brightest hours of the day. It actually felt safer that most roads I used during a typical day. The Highway 50 shoulder was wide, keeping Wilson and I far out of harm's way whenever the occasional car did pass by. These cars could also be seen from miles away across the unbroken darkness, which gave me plenty of time to react to them. In terms of weather, the night air had a slight chill to it, which was unheard of during any Kansas July day, and a blessing beyond words.

For as enjoyable as night hiking proved to be, I paid the price for it in when I resumed my walking late the following morning. The sudden switch in my walk/sleep cycle threw me for a serious loop. My legs begged for a break after just an hour or so of movement. They could normally go at least fifteen miles before any sort of fatigue began setting in. My eyes stung and longed to slam shut right then and there as I walked. I tried my best to stay upright and focused only on closing the distance to the rest area that sat a mile ahead.

I made it to the rest area at around 10:30 AM and called it a day. I was about to learn what it was like to spend an entire day at a rest area in rural Kansas. A solid nap would probably refresh me enough to permit a full afternoon of walking after I woke up, but it seemed unnecessary to strive for anything more than I'd already gotten done for the day. I didn't feel rushed to get anywhere. Colorado was a few days ahead, and I'd get there when I got there.

It wasn't the worst rest area I'd ever seen, but it certainly wasn't anything special. There was a building with restrooms, a map of the area, a drink machine, and an outdoor water faucet there. Next to the main building was a covered picnic table. I wheeled Wilson over into the shade of the covered table area, then went back to the soda machine. My only focus and care in the entire world was getting a cold can of Coke and drinking it. Had you asked me then, I would have said my entire life depended on it.

Pulling some loose change from my pocket, I put a quarter into the machine. Something didn't seem right. The rolling of the quarter through old machine's mechanisms and the metal-on-metal sound of the coin dinging home never came. I peered into the coin slot to notice it was plugged up. There were several coins jammed tightly in there. I tried to forcefully push another quarter into the slot and break up the blockage, but had no luck.

With my frustration building quickly, I rushed back over to Wilson, grabbed a knife, and hurriedly ran back to the machine. The thin butter knife would easily fit in the slot and hopefully dislodge the coins. While slowly sliding its blade into the slot, I noticed the knife was barely long enough for the job. While gripping the last centimeter of knife still visible outside of the slot, my sweaty fingers slipped, and in it went with a dull clink. There was no getting it out. My dreams of a cold Coke were dead. Life is a bitch sometimes. I looked up in despair to see a security camera about three feet from my face. It was definitely on, so I gave it a mean look and walked off, hoping that nobody ever checked the footage.

Sulking back at the picnic table, I took a big swig off my water jug. Its contents seemed to be well on the way to reaching a rolling boil after a morning in unobstructed sunlight. As I tried to find the motivation required to get up and fill the jug with cold water from the pump next to the rest area building, I noticed a truck pull into the parking area. Everyone in the truck was staring at me, especially the lady in the passenger seat. I tried my best to smile and waved at them. The lady waved back, got out of the truck, reached into its bed, and pulled something out of it. She then made her way toward me. I hoped that I didn't smell too badly as she approached.

She got close and said, "Would you like a drink?" as she handed me an ice cold can of Coke.

~

The remaining miles to Colorado passed easily. Places like Garden City and Lakin treated me well. In Syracuse, I was yet again welcomed in by a family that I'd never met like I was an old friend.

I was actually sad to leave Kansas — the same state everyone had warned me about like I would be walking through the gates of hell when I arrived there. The place certainly had its annoyances, from self-righteous religious fanatics to nosy and overtly paranoid townies who called the police on me every single damn day, but I liked it anyway. It did not rain a single time during my 21 days in Kansas, which in itself was enough to earn my affection after the way the Midwest had tried to drown me out. I cherished the easy walking, prairie sunsets, and generous small town folks. I would miss it all, from the Reinke showers to the quirky town welcoming signs. I would even think back fondly on the absurdity of the beef industry propaganda that could be seen almost anywhere. Southern Kansas is home to some of the largest cattle yards in the world. Not far from the Colorado border, a sign attached to a tall grain elevator that lorded over one of these vast cattle yards read: EAT BEEF – KEEP SLIM.

I also knew the landscape would soon become more challenging. The Rockies loomed ahead, which kept a tiny bit of fear planted in my mind at all times. I wasn't sure if I was quite ready for them yet. It wasn't long before the first glimpse into Colorado opened up in front of me. It was even flatter looking than Kansas. There would be no purple mountain majesties for me yet. No matter how hard I stared down the sagebrush wasteland ahead, no towering peaks manifested themselves.

Chapter 16: Forty Miles

I reached the city of Lamar the afternoon after entering Colorado. While walking to the city park and baseball fields to camp, I noticed a bicyclist on the other side of the road looking at me strangely. I waved. He waved back and came over to introduce himself.

His name was Mike. He was cycling across the country from San Francisco to New York. It turned out that we were heading for the same camping area. We arranged to meet there shortly, as he was making a small detour to grab some beers on the way.

When we met up later, Mike and I settled on camping in one of the many available dugouts at the park's softball and baseball fields. As we searched around for the best dugout in the park, Mike told me a little bit about himself. He was a Marine and had gotten out of the service a couple of years earlier. He had been all over the world during his time in the military, which included a tour of duty in one of the most dangerous areas of Afghanistan. He didn't talk about it much, and I got the feeling he didn't want to. All he really said about it was, "People don't realize what they have here."

Mike was an imposing figure at probably 6' 2" tall with a muscular build. He was also carrying a gun. I hadn't felt as safe in a camping situation since I slept in the police station parking lot way back in Madison, Indiana.

We found a suitable dugout and set our tents up inside it. As we talked over a couple of warm Bud Lights with the city lights barely brightening up our surroundings enough to see each other, I said, "I want to thank you for your service." He replied as any Marine would, "It's my honor."

~

I found myself in a small general store in the town of Hasty the following afternoon. There were a couple of foldable tables set up inside with newspapers spread across them, which looked like a good place to get some rest. The store's lone employee was an older lady who was taking care of a young child. The kid played happily in a shopping cart that was being used as a makeshift crib.

I asked the lady if I could sit down inside and hang out for a while to get out of the heat. She looked at me, smiled, and said, "Of course hun, everyone's welcome here."

I could not possibly explain to you how nice that was to hear. The odd way I was being looked at by people hadn't really changed much since the beginning of the walk, but it was finally starting to get to me. A person could only take so many mean looks and stares. I was tired of parents seeing me walking down the sidewalk toward them and pulling their kids in close. When some people saw me approaching their homes as they were going to their mailboxes, I noticed their paces quicken so they could get there and back without having to interact with me. Others crossed the street when they saw me coming toward them on the sidewalk. As much as I hated to admit it, these things hurt. Many people looked at me like I was nothing, like I wasn't even worth the small effort it would take to return my wave or friendly hello.

The good thing about all this negative stuff was that whenever it happened, more often than not, something encouraging would distract me from it soon after. My reception in the city of La Junta, Colorado was a perfect example of this. I was treated to a free hotel room and dinner by the La Junta tourism board. They contacted me out of the blue and insisted on making my time in their little city as comfortable as possible, which they succeeded at. I ate a delicious meal at a local restaurant, Jodi's Grill, and spent the rest of my time there in my motel room resting and route planning. The rest ended up being exactly what I needed, as things were about to get interesting. My first extended stretch of lonely desert walking lied ahead, but even that would have to wait for one serious clusterfuck of a day to be over.

    I left my motel room in La Junta the morning after my complimentary stay and happily strolled to a Safeway down the road. After buying some groceries, I noticed that Wilson was moving differently as we worked our way across the store's parking lot. The poor guy had a severe flat tire. It was so bad that I knew it could not be patched with the neon green, radioactive-looking tire slime I'd been using to fix flats for a while.

    Remembering there was a Wal-Mart up the road, I told the Safeway manager I was going to leave Wilson there and make the trek to Wal-Mart in search of solid rubber inner tubes for his tires. This was something I should have done much earlier. The walk to Wal-Mart ended up being a lengthy three miles each way. Once there, I pleaded out loud to the universe as I approached the bicycle section, desperately hoping that they would have the size of solid rubber inner tubes I needed. They did. I rejoiced. However, in my rejoicing, I was distracted from the fact that the tubes did not come in a two-pack, but were instead sold one at a time.

    I walked all the way back to the Safeway before noticing this. When I opened the package and realized I would have to walk the three miles to Wal-Mart and three miles back all over again, I was furious. I went into Safeway, bought an energy drink, and sat down outside next to my injured friend and told him how pissed I was.

Thankfully, the heart to heart with Wilson and caffeine lifted my spirits considerably, and I began the long march to Wal-Mart once again. The mid-morning temperature was a fiery 100 degrees. I made it to Wal-Mart and back in a couple of hours, and then began the task of getting the solid rubber tubes inside Wilson's tires. It did not happen easily, but they managed to fit after some straining and swearing.

There was a campground next to Wal-Mart that I had spotted on my second trip there, so I once again walked those three pesky miles to it and checked into a tidy little tent site. The lady at the campground's registration desk was pleasant and gave me a discount. The cost for the site was still too expensive, but I badly needed a place to relax. I went into Wal-Mart for the third time of the day, bought a big bottle of beer, and sat down at my overpriced site's picnic table.

I had walked over 15 miles during the course of the day, but was still in the same town I had started walking in that morning. In fact, I was further from my actual route than when I had begun. I had walked negative miles for the day. Feeling discouraged, I downed my bottle of beer and jumped in the campground pool. I then caught up on a couple of my favorite TV shows over the campground's Wi-Fi as I drip dried in the day's last rays of sun. I'd say that it was a combination of those things that made me feel better, but it was mostly just the beer.

As I prepared to end my day and get some sleep, I decided I would begin an exciting quest in the morning — a quest for a new personal record of miles walked in a day. My current record sat at right around 31 miles. I'd known since the beginning of the walk that I wanted to walk 40 miles in a day, and decided the time was right to go for it. It seemed like a reasonable yet still highly challenging distance to chase after. As usual, I had no idea what I was getting myself into.

~

In case you aren't aware, 40 miles is a long way to walk in a day. I knew I'd have to start early, so I made sure I was on the road by 7 AM and making my way to Colorado Route 10, a remote strip of cracked asphalt with nothing but far off cattle ranches and high desert plains for 73 miles to Walsenburg. The sun was relentless even in the early morning hours.

When I reached Route 10, I saw a mile marker with the number 73 on it. I decided I would not stop walking until I reached mile marker 33. I had already walked 1.5 miles to get there, so it would be a 41.5 mile day. My plan was to walk steadily all day with few breaks and to eat and drink while moving as much as possible. Caffeine coursed through my veins as I tackled the day's first mile. It felt too easy. I had already consumed a NOS Energy and had one more ready to go, along with a can of Mountain Dew. It was certainly enough caffeine to make a person hear their heart beating, but I was just hoping it was also enough to keep a person's legs moving well after they had reached their maximum level of exertion, as well as keep their mind buzzed enough to think that walking 40+ miles was a fun idea. Wilson was filled to capacity with food, which included a few calorie-packed military MRE meals and an arrangement of other treats. It would be an experiment in human endurance, stupidity, and caffeine.

I felt fairly confident in the plan. The only thing that made me nervous was that Wilson hadn't been watching his diet closely enough and weighed about 100 pounds. I hoped the lay of the land would be as flat as I anticipated it would be. Luckily, it was. I made encouraging progress right out of the gate. By early afternoon I had already walked a little over 20 miles.

Right around the 20 mile mark, I crested a small ridge and was startled by what I saw. There was a baby jogger sitting on the side of the road. It looked a lot like Wilson. It surprised me because there were really no homes on Route 10, as it was all empty ranch land. I looked around and there was nobody in sight, so I approached the stroller slowly. As I peered around the side of it that was facing away from me, I noticed a man sitting on the ground and leaning his back up against it. He was sound asleep. He was wearing all black, including long black leggings underneath his black shorts and a long-sleeved black shirt. After a few attempts at waking him up with no luck, the stranger finally shot to life and stood up quickly. I had frightened him. When you're traveling on foot with a baby stroller in such a remote place, the last thing you expect to see is another person doing the same thing.

His name was Kay. He was doing a run around the world and was in the process of getting his run across North America done. I can't remember exactly where he had already run, but it was inspiring nonetheless. Kay was from Japan, but spoke English better than many of the people I met throughout the Midwest (ok, maybe that's not saying much), and was running about 35 miles a day. We laughed for a bit about meeting each other in such an odd place. I figured that if Kay could run 35 miles every single day, I could walk 41.5 once.

Something interesting happened later in the afternoon. I saw mountains. The Sangre De Cristo range, a subrange of the Rockies, suddenly appeared through distant clouds. They were towering peaks that stuck out like sore thumbs above the high desert nothingness. It was an incredible sight. I'd never seen the mountains of The West in such a meaningful setting. I'd seen them on my road trip out to Portland on my mini walk vacation, but that was out the window of a car, for the most part. These mountains, these monsters ahead, I had walked to from sea level over the course of about four million steps.

Despite the adrenaline boost that came from seeing the mountains, I lost every ounce of energy I had at the day's 32 mile mark. The walking was easy enough, but it was unbearably hot on the pavement. There was almost no shade off Route 10, so I was using my umbrella for some shelter from the sun during my short breaks. I sat down and ate one of the MRE's my grandmother sent me. The 1,200 or so fast calories gave me an immediate boost, so I pushed onward. It was only a few miles before I hit a wall again. I leaned on Wilson and thought about giving up. Nightfall was well on its way.

When you're doing something excruciatingly difficult, you sometimes have to take a few moments to reflect on why you're doing it. This seems obvious, but these reasons can become blurred after a while when you are so wrapped up in your task that you forget how to do anything else, including think. So there I sat — dehydrated, exhausted, and thinking about why I wanted to walk 40 miles. I returned to a well-used and wildly effective source of inspiration, which was considering how some people probably thought I'd never make it as far as I had on the walk. I had stood in the Atlantic Ocean, started walking, and there I was looking at the Rocky Mountains. They could all go to hell. I had to do it. Plus, if I did, my friend Joel would owe me 40 beers thanks to a bet made months earlier. I thought about the beers a lot during those last five miles, and how much I would enjoy Joel losing the bet.

It was well after dark by the time I finally reached mile marker 33. I felt energized for a moment after seeing it, but the initial rush soon waned as I felt myself falling asleep right where I stood. It was the kind of sleep that you can't fend off no matter how hard you try. You either give in and lay down, or hope that you don't fall on something sharp or hard when your eyes close for the last time without you even knowing it and you collapse to the ground. I hobbled about 20 feet off the road, set up my tent in the darkness without using my flashlight, crawled inside it, and passed out.

I woke up once during the night to bright lights outside my tent. A car was stopped on the road, just parked there and not moving at all. I realized how potentially dangerous the situation could be, as I was unarmed and there was not another person within 40 miles besides whoever was in the car. I thought about this for a moment, then rolled over and went back to sleep. Whoever it was could have gotten out and murdered me and I wouldn't have even tried to stop them. Sleep had officially become more of a priority than staying alive. The car must have left eventually, as I am not dead right now and it wasn't there when I awoke, but I never heard or saw it drive away.

Chapter 17: As Long As The Bears Don't Get Me

I felt sore as I arose in the morning and dug my toes into the cool dirt outside my tent. I hadn't been sore in quite a while. The realization that Walsenburg, my next resupply point, was still about 33 miles away scared me. I had the lofty goal of getting across Route 10 in two days, but it didn't feel like that was going to happen as I limped around on legs that felt like sand bags. The biggest problem was that I had eaten at least two days worth of food and drank three gallons of water during the 40 mile walk, so supplies were low. At the very least I had to get close enough to Walsenburg that it would only be a short walk away the following morning, as I'd likely be completely out of food and water by then.

I managed to walk 24 miles in about 12 hours during the day. It was an uncharacteristically poor showing. Those 40 miles had taken more of a toll on my body than I had anticipated they would. I camped on the side of the road and could see Walsenburg in the valley below from my spot, just a short nine miles away. I had limited water and only a couple of Pop-Tarts and some potato chips left for food, but I figured it would be enough to get me to town in the morning. The sun was going down as the mountains and the clouds around them turned to shades of purple and dark red. A lightning storm came in from the west and pummeled the town below as I sat on the hill and watched.

After making it to Walsenburg the next morning on nothing but fumes, I headed out of town to find a place to camp. I got to Lathrop State Park after just a few miles of walking, set up camp, and took a shower. There was a bicycling crew made up of about a dozen high school kids camping there as well. They were all pedaling across the country together on their summer breaks. They gave me seven hot dogs, all of which I ate within a few minutes, then I sat with them at their end of the day sharing time. Everyone in the group shared the high and low points of their days. I said my low point was getting rained on in the morning, and my high point was meeting them and their gift of seven hot dogs.

The following morning, I began my ascent into the Sangre De Cristos. Walking up the range wasn't too strenuous. There was a wide shoulder on the road and its grade was reasonably gradual most of the way. The mountains were stunning, with green forested sides and bald tops. I decided to stop for the day just short of the North La Veta Pass summit, elevation 9,413 feet, and prepared myself for my first night of camping in the high Colorado mountains. I recorded a video and said, "Life is real good, as long as the bears don't get me."

~

In the chilled morning air I quickly made the five miles to North La Veta summit after a nippy night in the tent. After celebrating up there and marveling at the sights, I began my leisurely descent. Things evened out into a sort of high elevation plateau. The landscape opened up, a wide pasture appeared to my left. The forest surrounding the pasture was lush. I looked out into the pasture to admire it, directed my vision back to the road ahead, then looked back to the pasture suddenly, hoping that what I thought I had just seen was an illusion of some kind. A hint of movement near the tree line about 200 yards away had caught my eye. Sadly, I was not mistaken.

There was a bear running full speed directly at me.

"Oh, shit."

The bear kept coming.

I froze without the slightest idea of what to do. It kept coming faster and faster. I think I would have rather been charged from 20 feet than 200 yards. The seconds dragged on and on as the bear kept gaining speed and decreasing the distance between us. The waiting was agonizing, even if it was for my own death.

Suddenly the bear took a slight turn away from me as it reached the halfway point between the clearing's tree line and myself. It was not far enough away so I was in the clear, but far enough to slow down the rapidly approaching moment when I would piss myself (in case you're wondering, I didn't). Now at this time, instead of trying to get my walking stick out of Wilson to fight back should the bear change its mind or find some place to hide, I decided to grab my camera and snap a photo. It was an action so strange that I'm not even going to try to make sense of it. So I took a blurry, out-of-focus photo of the hairy assassin. Of course, the second after I did this, the bear paused for a moment, looked at me, then corrected its path and began accelerating toward me once again at full throttle.

The beast came to a screeching halt once it hit the cattle fence to my left, which sat about 100 feet away. I puffed out my chest and tried to look as big as I could and yelled, "Stay there! Stay! Stay there you fucker!"

The bear put its front paws up on the top rung of the cattle fence and stared at me for a few seconds. The fence was buckling under its weight, which I would guess was between 300-400 pounds. I stared right back into the bear's eyes and kept yelling as loud as I could manage to.

Then, in one incredibly swift and athletic movement, the bear hopped the fence and made its way up to the road and directly toward me.

So there we were, man and bear, standing 40 feet from one another on the gravel road shoulder. It was a face off if I'd ever been in one. I knew the bear could cover that 40 feet and be right on top of me before I could even move or let out a final scream.

I'm not sure how much time passed as we stood there sizing each other up. I had no protection but my own appearance, so I tried to seem intimidating. This is not easy to do when you're a malnourished and scrawny hiker. I flailed around and kept up the constant yelling. The bear stood its ground and stayed locked right on my eyes.

As this was going down, a truck appeared around the corner ahead, then drove slowly by the bear and up to me. I waved frantically for the driver to stop. He gave me a friendly wave back and continued on his way. Incensed, I could not believe that he didn't stop. A car then pulled up behind me, so I turned around to try the same thing again. The driver snapped a picture with their camera and continued right on past the bear and me. I was dumbfounded by the stupidity of these people and overflowing with rage, but didn't have time to try and chase them down to give them a piece of my mind. There was a bear 40 feet from me.

I turned back to my challenger. The beast looked meaner than ever. After a few more seconds of the stare down, however, the bear committed to doing something other than just standing there and scaring the shit out of me, and bolted. And thank God or Allah or evolution or whatever that it chose to sprint up the hill across the road instead of at Wilson and myself.

I wasted no time in getting as far away as I could after the bear took off. I looked back in fear as I scrambled down the road, afraid the bear would change its mind once again. On a few of these paranoid gazes backward, I could see it standing on the hillside watching me.

I don't know if I was more scared about what had just happened or angry with the two motorists who simply stood by and watched as I endured the most frightening situation of my life, but I was frantic. It's good that neither of the two drivers came back, because I would have killed them. No joke.

After what seemed like an eternity, I made it to a turnoff down Highway 160. There was a trucker and another guy in a beat up pickup there talking to each other. I walked up to them and said, "I just got charged by a bear just up the road, any chance you have bear spray or anything to keep me safe until I get to town since I'm walking? The bear still has its eyes on me. I saw it on the hillside."

The beat up truck guy looked at me and said, "Bears? Just stay away from the bears," with a condescending *I'm a Colorado native* tone.

"That's very helpful, thanks," I said, then walked off before I took my frustration out on the local asshole. I practically ran the ten or so miles to the nearest town, Fort Garland, then set up camp and braced for the bear themed nightmares that were inevitably coming my way once my eyes closed for the day.

What haunted me most about the ordeal was the aggressiveness of the bear, as well as its physical features. It had a thicker neck than I had ever seen on a black bear and its fur was light brown. I had actually been charged by a black bear once before during a hiking trip in Vermont some years earlier, and the situation then felt much different than what had just happened. The Vermont black bear had been a mother with cubs, so she should have easily been the meanest bear I'd ever encountered. She reacted swiftly, but appropriately. I was, albeit unknowingly, too close to her cubs. But this Colorado bear had a blood curdling, menacing look about it that I couldn't quite shake from my memory. It was aggressive in a way that did not seem typical, and came at me completely unprovoked from a distance that any bear expert or experienced outdoorsman would deem to be more than far enough away to not only be safe, but likely entirely free of the risk of inciting a charge. Things just didn't seem to add up. The first thing that came to mind as I considered all of this was that it might have been a grizzly. They usually attack less frequently than black bears, but typically with much greater ferocity when they do. I knew that grizzlies technically did not exist in Colorado at all, but had been hearing stories from locals about their supposed existence that made me consider thinking otherwise. I was especially familiar with the tale of one famous grizzly that was killed in a relatively close-by area of San Juan National Forest in 1979. When that bear was killed, no grizzly sightings had been confirmed in Colorado during the previous 25 years. The 1979 griz had been an old sow, which biologists determined had given birth to cubs during her life. None of her cubs were ever located.

 A couple of days after the charging, I had the opportunity to show the photo I took of the bear to a Rio Grande National Forest ranger. I made sure to watch his reaction to the photo closely, as I hadn't told him what it was of prior to showing it to him. I simply asked, "Can you check out this photo for me?" I handed him the camera, and he got a curious look on his face. He said, "Well, huh."

"What does that mean?" I asked with a laugh.

"Well, it's either a big black bear or a young grizzly," he replied. It was shocking to hear a Colorado forest ranger say the word "grizzly" and be serious about it. What was confusing him, as well as me, was the thickness of the bear's neck. It appeared to have the makings of a hump, which is a telltale sign of a grizzly. The bear's color was also a light-brown/cinnamon color. "I technically can't tell you they exist, but the locals around here, especially up near the pass where you were, swear that they do," he said about grizzlies as he handed me back my camera.

The ranger went on to tell me something about black bears that I had never been aware of before, which was that their fur could turn a light cinnamon-brown color during certain parts of the year. When I heard that, I decided in my mind that it was a black bear I had dealt with. The fat neck and extreme aggressiveness didn't matter much to me anymore. I didn't want it to be a grizzly, so it didn't have to be. It probably wasn't anyway. All I cared about was that I was still alive.

~

Coming up ahead was the Continental Divide at Wolf Creek Pass. It was getting progressively colder each night, which was a point of concern because of my lack of winter gear. I had gotten rid of much of it once spring arrived back east. The timing for my topping of the Rockies was such that I would have to camp around 10,000 feet of elevation for at least one night. I hoped the gear I did have would work well enough to keep me out of danger and began my climb into the mountains.

My ascent began around the town of South Fork, where I spent a night at a campground before practically dashing toward the peaks of the San Juan Mountains in the morning. The going was not as steep as I anticipated it would be, at least for the first part of the day. I met an energetic group of bicyclists near the bottom of the pass. They were from Lizard Head Cycling, an adventure bicycle trip company. We talked for a while and they gave me a couple of apples to eat. Members of the group passed me every few minutes as we all made our way up the great incline. They shouted words of encouragement as they pedaled past me. I cheered them on right back. I decided I was much happier walking than I would be cycling. Several of the group's members looked pretty miserable. They were sweating and struggling as I leisurely pushed Wilson at a comfortable pace. I admired them all a lot for taking on the hill in such a way.

Like my first Rockies pass at La Veta, Wolf Creek wasn't overly challenging physically. It was at least 11 or 12 miles of constant up, but my body was well conditioned and handled it all in stride. Just another day's work. The road wound up into serene fir forests as a consistent yet light and manageable drizzle of rain came down. There were a few tunnels along the route, which usually posed quite a lot of trouble for Wilson and I, but the first two had sidewalks in them. A heavy rain storm decided to stir up some trouble as I was inside the second tunnel, so I sat down on its sidewalk and enjoyed a snack while waiting for the saturated clouds above to pass. I thought about the fact that once I topped the summit ahead, the same rainwater that was pouring down outside of the mouth of the tunnel in front of me would be bound for the Pacific ocean, just as I was. That was a neat thought.

The third tunnel did not have a large shoulder, and I narrowly missed getting hit by a car inside it. The only other problem during the ascent, aside from the near collision in the last tunnel, came in the form of a short period of altitude sickness at around 10,000 feet, which hit me just a short distance from the summit. All it took was a few minutes of rest, some food, and a big dose water to get me back to my normal self, then I pressed onward.

Soon I was standing at 10,857 feet. I had reached the Continental Divide. There wasn't much of a view to speak of because of a blanket of dense high mountain fog. It was pretty flat up there on top of the range. A deer wandered without the slightest worry through a small meadow nearby. I eyed the tree line for charging bears, none came my way. As I stood on top of the Rockies in the fog, I took some time to consider what I had just done. I looked at Wilson and said, "Wil', this is a long way from Delaware."

I took a few pictures and enjoyed the scenery, but didn't hang around for too long. The sun was going down, so I had to find a secure camping place at the lowest elevation possible. I ended up finding a place just off a national forest road that was not only flat and dry, but right next to a gorgeous waterfall. It sat at around 10,000 feet.

My phone rang as I was eating my dinner. It was one of the folks from the Lizard Head Cycling crew calling. They invited me to join the whole gang for dinner in Pagosa Springs the following evening. I smiled as I ate my cold ravioli. It felt nice to know I wouldn't have to eat it again the next night. The constant rushing of the waterfall put me to sleep quickly. It was July, but still cold enough outside that I could see my breath in my tent before I dozed off.

~

    I walked into Pagosa Springs the next afternoon after negotiating many miles of steep switchbacks. Pagosa looked like an idyllic Rocky Mountain town. The San Juan River flowed right through the middle of it. Hordes of people were beating the heat by tubing down the river and relaxing on its banks as I passed by. A constant slope of evergreen led out of town and up to distant metamorphic peaks.
    My first stop in Pagosa Springs was at The Springs Resort and Spa. My host connection in town, Sheilah, worked at the resort. I had never met Sheilah before, but she was a friend of a friend back in Maine, where she was originally from.
    Sheilah was energetic and welcoming, just as I had expected from my friend's description of her. I struggled getting Wilson into her car, or "cah" as she said it. I was thrilled to hear a Maine accent again. Sheilah had a convertible Chrysler Sebring, and Wilson had to be nearly fully dismantled to fit awkwardly into its back seat, which he finally did after some maneuvering. Once Wilson was squared away, Sheilah got me into the hot springs at the resort for free. I soaked in a variety of pools with temperature choices ranging from 83 to 114 degrees. Many of the pools offered views of the San Juan River below.
    I met the Lizard Head Cycling crew for dinner at the Alley House Grille in Pagosa later in the evening. We all shared stories from our respective trips and enjoyed delicious meals. The place had a fairly pricey menu, so as usual, I felt uncomfortable ordering such expensive

food. Everyone in the group was in their 40s or 50s and from a wide range of different backgrounds. They peddled all day together, then stopped at nice hotels and ate fancy meals to reward their hard work. I, of course, traveled in the exact opposite manner as that. They seemed to get a kick out of how out of my element I was at the restaurant. We all drank a bit and ended up having a hell of a time. When I left, they gave me a bunch of cash and wished me luck. I promised I'd put them in my book if I wrote one.

The next day took me past Chimney Rock, a famous natural monument that lords over San Juan National Forest. It is really nothing more than just a big rock that looks sort of like a chimney. Americans seem to be fascinated by this vague resemblance. You can find a Chimney Rock in North Carolina, Nebraska, Arizona, Washington, and Utah. While still within sight of the beloved monolith, I walked by a house with a big red barn next to it. It was a beautiful barn, so I stopped to admire it. There was a lady in the house's yard watering some plants, which I had not noticed. She called to me and waved, then made her way over to say hi.

"You're Nate!" she said with a huge smile on her face as she approached.

"I am! And how do you know that?"

Her name was Jane. It turned out that she worked with Sheilah at the resort. Sheilah had told her all about me, and she had been wondering if I'd be wandering by. She invited me into her house for a cold drink. Jane lived with her husband, Matt, along with their daughter, son-in-law, and infant grandson. I had only been in the house for a few minutes before Jane offered me a place to stay on the property for the night. There was a camper behind the house that I could stay in.

Jane was exceedingly happy all the time. She always had a look on her face that made it seem like she absolutely couldn't wait to hear what I had to say. Matt showed up at the house soon after I did. He was soft spoken, but had an aura of authority about him. I instantly figured he had been in the military. Sure enough, I learned he had been for over 30 years.

The road between Matt and Jane's house and Durango, my next major stop, was a nightmare. Its shoulders were narrow and the traffic on it was constant and fast moving. I stayed with Matt and Jane for several days as they transported me back and forth between my daily starting and ending points. Because of this, I only had to carry a daypack, which helped me avoid the dangers of pushing Wilson along the sketchy roads.

Matt and Jane made sure to tell me God was watching out for me. They were the most religious people I had ever met, devout in a way I actually envied a little bit. On my last morning with them, Matt and Jane said they wanted to anoint Wilson with oil from Israel. They prayed and put tiny dabs of fragrant oil on his handle and wheels. Whether I believed in the power of the oil or not, it was a supremely kind gesture.

Matt told me stories from his time in the military during our final drive together to the outskirts of Durango, where my unsupported journey would begin again. As we arrived at the gas station that would be my starting point for the day, he said, "Thanks so much for listening to all my stories."

"It's been my pleasure, Matt. I'm glad I got to hear them."

"Well, thanks. I have to say, your parents really raised you right."

"They really did, or they at least tried their best with two boys who liked to cause trouble," I said back with a laugh. We exchanged goodbyes and I was off on my own again. What Matt said about my parents made me miss them. I called each of them before leaving the gas station.

~

There wasn't too much of Colorado left to be walked once I got through Durango. Utah was fast approaching. There were more mountains ahead, but they were all relatively easy to pass over. The landscape opened up and seemed friendlier and less likely to kill me.

Dove Creek was my last stop in Colorado. I got permission to camp in one of the town parks there, and set up my tent in the early evening. As I sat at a picnic table reading the daylight away, a man walked toward me from the other side of the park. He was old and scruffy looking. He also had a massive parrot perched on his shoulder.

"Heya," he said as he sat across from me at my picnic table.

"Hey, nice parrot."

"Thanks. This is Yoyo. He's 18 years old," he said as Yoyo reached his head down and gave his owner's hand a swift chomp.

"Damnit, Yoyo!" the man screamed.

We talked for a while and he told me about growing up in the area. He shared that he had a 75 mile commute to work every day, among other little tidbits of information about his life. He was an underground mechanic or something like that.

"Times is hard, I'll tell ya. But that's just the way it is," he said as he took a last drag off his cigarette, grinned at me, and walked off. Yoyo sat happily on his shoulder and bent his head down to bite him every now and then as they moved at a slow pace across the park. His frequent scolding of Yoyo's bad behavior faded off in volume as he disappeared down a side street. I was glad I had gotten to talk to someone before the day ended. Admittedly, the conversation was a bit on the bland side, but I was deeply thankful for it anyway, as each day seemed to be just a bit lonelier than the one before it. The towns were getting smaller, the distances between them longer. Conversations were becoming just as valuable to me as anything else, even the dull ones.

Chapter 18: Martian Dirt

After crossing into Utah, I made my way through the rather unremarkable towns of Monitello and Blanding uneventfully, and Utah State Route 95 was up next. Route 95 was recommended to me by Mike, the Marine bicyclist I camped with in the baseball dugout back in Colorado. He said it was the best road he'd ever been on. I was immediately intrigued by his description of the place, so I headed directly for it after we parted ways. The only problem with 95 was that it was proving to be a bit of a logistical struggle as I prepared for it. For 122 miles, the road offered almost nothing except for a long strip of pavement that wove through seemingly endless dry desert valleys and red rock canyons. Beautiful scenery, sure, but scenery alone can't sustain a weary walker. There was one campground with a general store and water about 60 miles in, but that was it. Not a single residential property sat along the route. It was all open cattle range and BLM land. The Glen Canyon area, which most of Route 95 is contained within, was among the last places in the entire United States to be surveyed and mapped because of its inhospitable landscape. I felt nervous, but could not wait to begin.

This beginning took place in brushy desert. The road wound downward for miles on a constant and steep grade into a wide valley. Flanking the sides of the valley were oddly shaped rock formations and mesas. The mesas showcased a spectacular geologic cross-section. Thousands of horizontal slivers of rock stacked atop one another displayed every shade of orange and tan imaginable.

The first day on 95 went beautifully. I was calmed by the serenity of everything around me. There was almost no traffic on the road, maybe one car per hour on average. The walking was steep in places, but being in such a secluded place relaxed my mind to the point that everything physical was on autopilot. I felt as if I was gliding through the canyons. With very little attention needing to be paid to the road because of the virtually nonexistent traffic, my head was on a swivel, just amazed at the beauty that had been created by nothing more than some water and the simple passing of time. I don't believe in much, but I do believe in erosion.

　　I made my way up a steep incline and directly into the east side of Cedar Mesa in the late afternoon. Cedar Mesa occupies roughly 400 square miles of land in southeastern Utah, and I was going to explore a tiny section of it around Grand Gulch, and more specifically, Comb Wash. The road had been blasted directly through a part of the mesa. The resulting sandstone cliffs that rose up on each side of the road swallowed me up. I shouted loudly, my voice returning to my ears in a series of echoes.

　　As I emerged from the mesa I found myself in the most breathtaking nature setting of the walk so far. Every corner of the road on 95 wowed me more than the previous one. The scene after this particular corner was like something off a post card or a National Geographic feature. The mesa stretched out as far as I could see to my right and left. It was light orange and had sage bushes lining its top and bottom. The road through the valley was curvy and looked like a cowboy's whip frozen in mid-air. Comb Wash, which was filled with eroded rocks, low shrubs, and patches of tall cottonwoods, laid out for about a mile directly in front of me to the next incline, and for endless miles to the west. It was unspeakably stunning.

Life On Foot

I stopped to camp at a BLM site down in Comb Wash. To my surprise and sheer joy, there was another guy there. I went up to him and introduced myself immediately. His name was Cam. Cam was an archaeologist and on vacation. He was exploring the rich archaeological area that was Grand Gulch — an archaeologist on vacation doing archaeology work. He reminded me of my dad in the way that my dad goes fishing on his days off from work, even though his job is to guide people on fishing trips. Some people really have it all figured out.

Cam invited me to come over to his site anytime for a beer, which I did once my things were set up nearby. We walked around the campsite area looking for ancient Pueblo pottery pieces. He had already found a couple of them before I arrived. Cam had eyes like an eagle and was finding the 1,000+ year old pottery sherds with ease. I became frustrated when he had found six pieces and I hadn't yet found a single one. Finally, my luck changed and I found a piece of what Cam called gray ware, as well as two more colorful pieces that he called black-on-red. The black-on-red ones fascinated me. They were made of a blood red clay base and painted with dark paint that had faded considerably over the centuries, but could still be seen easily. One piece had squiggly lines and the other had straight ones. It was strangely thrilling to find such old relics on my own and hold onto them. They were not in a museum, but real objects that someone had held in their own hands and labored over ten centuries before I was even born.

We scattered the pieces around the same area we found them in once we were done searching around. Cam warned me that taking ancient Pueblo artifacts of any kind was a good way to get yourself cursed. He told me of Pueblo ruin robbers who would mysteriously go mad and kill themselves after stealing priceless artifacts from the surrounding canyons.

The evening sky soon turned purple. Shortly after that, the moon rose over the mesa. It illuminated Comb Wash to the point that a flashlight was not necessary to move around. I wandered about in the moonlight for some time, then Cam and I sat down at his picnic table and got drunk.

~

I explored some Pueblo ruins further up Route 95 the next day. It was time to put the skills Cam taught me to the test. I found more gray ware and a large piece of black-on-white, and was very pleased with myself for doing so.

The Blue Mountains appeared behind me later on as I topped yet another steep incline. I stopped to relieve myself right on the side of the road after looking both ways down it and seeing no vehicles in sight. I'm honestly not sure why I even bothered to look, as the traffic was so consistently sparse. So there I stood, completely exposed on top of a hill. As I stood there, I took in my surroundings from left to right. Blue Mountains, wide desert plain, craggy red rocks, weather observation camera pointed directly at me. Damn, I was on camera. I smiled and gave the camera an awkward little wave, finished my business, then simply walked off, wondering all the while if someone in a room full of video monitors, or perhaps a live audience through an online feed somewhere, had just watched me pee.

I saw a deep canyon gouged out of white rocks ahead, a sort of canyon within a canyon. Its walls were steep and porous. Years of erosion had carved holes ranging in size from pebbles to school buses down its sides. Rising mountains came into view then disappeared quickly as I rounded corners and found myself enclosed yet again in the network of tall mesas and buttes.

I camped amongst the red rocks. There was reddish-orange dirt all over everything I owned. It caked onto my socks and bare feet when I removed my shoes and walked around. It got into my sleeping bag and all over my arms and neck somehow. I felt like I was becoming part of the desert. It was eerily quiet at night along 95. I could hear mice scurrying around from far away. It was the kind of quiet that was so quiet I could hear the quiet, if that makes any sense. I had never in my life been in such a wild place.

Eventually I made it to the Hite Recreation Area of Glen Canyon. To get there I walked from a high plateau down into an intensely foreign environment. I'd grown accustomed to the desert, but this stretch was barren beyond anything I'd seen. It felt like I was walking on Mars. I pretended that I was wearing a spacesuit and reported back to some Earthlings through an imaginary radio transmitter. These are the things the desert does to you.

There was a general store at Hite, as well as cheap camping options right on the shore of Lake Powell. Lake Powell was gross. The water had a green tinge to it and smelled rotten. Regardless, I went swimming in it several times. I found a little cove to relax in, where I spent the afternoon soaking in the lake and then laying out on the warm rocks to dry off. I was camping near where the Dirty Devil and Colorado rivers converge into the northern tip of Lake Powell.

Stinky water aside, my campsite was perfect. There was a clean water fountain, a bathroom, and a store close by, but I was always just a short walk away from being isolated in the dry red dirt, exploring caves and canyons or dipping myself in the dirty yet still refreshing water. All of this was enjoyed for a whopping $7 per night. If there had been phone service there, I may have just stopped and become a permanent resident.

I stayed for two days and nights at Hite. During my last night there, I was very intent on having a few beers and lying on my picnic table to watch the stars. The sky was so clear at night that if I laid down in the right place, it felt like I was just floating around in space.

I bought a six-pack of Corona at the general store, which was great, but the store closed at around 7:00 PM, and it wasn't even close to dark at that point. Because of this, I had to buy a temporary cardboard cooler and ice. For a six-pack of beer it ended up costing me about $25, but it was worth it. I made a fire and drank my beer while talking to four German tourists I had met earlier and invited over to hang out. They were all guys about my age.

The Germans were a confusing bunch. All four of them slept in a cramped two-person tent. They didn't appear to have any camping gear other than the tent, and I believe they just slept in blankets and cozied up together. They had all finished university and were taking a gap year of sorts before entering their professional careers as doctors and scientists. They blabbed on about jobs and school and stuff like that. I tired of their company quickly, as they were boring beyond belief. I found myself actually falling asleep due to the dullness of their conversation. Thankfully, they retired early to their mini tent. With the Germans gone,

I finished my last beer, laid on my picnic table, and ventured off into the Milky Way.

~

There were a couple more days of walking between Hite and Hanksville, which was the town that marked the end of Route 95. The road became especially challenging in certain areas west of Hite. I regularly found myself at high elevations with expansive views over the reaching desert plain.

It rained hard one day, so I found shelter in a cave off the side of the road that had been carved out from the bottom of a fat mesa. I ate a can of beans and watched as the rain poured down the cave opening just a few feet in front of me. Once the rain did finally stop, I continued on, as the road became a maze amongst the rocks. It was all quite disorienting and frustrating for a while. I found it extremely difficult to judge distances in the network of cavernous canyons and sharp turns.

As I was zoning out and doing some zombie-like autopilot walking, a couple of bicyclists approached me. They were a father and daughter duo. The daughter said, "You're Nate aren't you?"

I said yes, to which she replied, "Josh is in Hanksville. He told us to look for you out here."

"Josh is in Hanksville!" I exclaimed. I thanked them for the message and they pedaled away, disappearing back into the Martian land.

Josh was a fellow wanderer I connected with initially back in Illinois when he called me to ask a few questions about walking across the country. Unlike most of the people who got in touch with me about walking, Josh actually decided to do it. He had walked almost exclusively to Indiana from Maryland, then began hitchhiking quite a bit from there, while still walking some as well.

Before losing phone service when I hit Route 95, I had sent Josh a brief message saying I was going to be ending up in Hanksville, and that he could meet me there if he wanted to. I thought that he was relatively close by in Colorado somewhere, which turned out to be true. I didn't expect him to actually do it at all, but apparently he was in Hanksville awaiting my arrival and ready to join me for an unspecified amount of time. I had never met Josh before, but had a feeling that we had a lot in common and would both enjoy some company for a while.

As my last evening on the road before reaching Hanksville approached, the Henry Mountains appeared and dominated the horizon. Storm clouds rolled over their summits but seemed content to stay up there, as the valley stayed dry and warm below. I set up camp just over a small roadside mound of orange dirt with a full view of the Henrys directly ahead. Dinner was eaten as the last rays disappeared behind the bald peaks.

The walking was flat and hot the next morning, obviously. About four or five miles from Hanksville, I became concerned. I felt like I should have been seeing some signs of life, but saw nothing except desolation. Ahead was an intimidating spread of mountains and buttes and deserted places. After being overly concerned about this for an unreasonably long amount of time, probably out of nothing but sheer boredom, I slowly began descending into a valley. Some scattered buildings came into view. I had made it to Hanksville.

With the little bit of phone service I had, I texted Josh as I got into town. A skinny figure soon appeared on the road ahead and waved. It was nice to see someone who looked as disheveled, sunburned, and insane as me. He had lots of tattoos, a lip piercing, his jeans were torn and had patches sewn onto them, and he wore a couple of long leather necklaces, one with a massive talon carved from some sort of white stone hanging off it. A ragged black bandana was tied loosely around his neck. We made our way to the Red Rock Restaurant and Campground, which was placed centrally in town. Josh was already well established there and had been for several days while waiting for me. I set my tent up on the campground area's green grass and walked around barefoot.

As the sun was going down, Josh and I walked to a store, which was built right into the side of one of the many crumbling hills in Hanksville. We bought beer and cigars, then scrambled to the top of yet another hill in the darkness to drink and smoke and tell stories from our adventures. The moon and stars were beaming in the typical Utah way. Josh shared thrilling stories of hitchhiking and living with the homeless wherever he went. He was a strong believer in Jesus, striving to live like him by showing love and compassion to the people most of society ignored. He spoke with those few others spoke to, shared meals with them, and let them know that he cared. Josh was dirty, nearly broke, smoked, drank, and sported many tattoos, but was as good of an example of Christian living as I could think of. After a couple of hours of getting acquainted, we settled on heading west in the morning. Before retiring to my tent, I made a trip to the campground's shower building. It had been a long, dirty trip down 95. Burnt orange pools of water collected around my feet on the shower floor.

Chapter 19: Why Have Just One?

The mission for the next day was to make it 17 miles to Caineville and find a place to camp there. The landscape was bone dry west of Hanksville. The red rocks and scattered shrubs disappeared, replaced by a mass of gray dirt and rock. The ground was cracked and looked like it hadn't seen any sort of moisture in years, or maybe ever. Then, seemingly out of nowhere, we wandered into a fertile valley bursting with plant life and crops. Occupying a large portion of this oasis was Mesa Farms Market, an organic farm with an accompanying store. Josh and I walked into the store anxious for a cold drink. They had fresh bread, produce, goat cheese, milk, and all sorts of other delicious looking items for sale.

Upon entering the market we found ourselves in a strange social situation. The man working there, whom we learned was the owner and operator of the farm, greeted us warmly. He asked how we were doing, commented on the weather, all that good stuff. This would all be normal, of course, except that he was laying flat on his back directly in the middle of the store while doing it. He seemed pretty determined to stay down there. We didn't really know what to do as we shifted around the room awkwardly for a couple minutes, but eventually just settled on talking to him as if he was standing. We got closer and stood over him as we chatted.

Finally, I had to ask. "What are you doing on the floor?"

"Oh, helps my back!" he said like he hadn't even realized anything was out of the ordinary.

Josh and I both ordered cantaloupe smoothies, then sat and talked with another young guy who worked at the farm underneath the glorious shade of the farm stand's front porch. Drinking that smoothie was not only one of the most enjoyable food related experiences of my life, but experiences in general. It was nothing but a nearly liquid cantaloupe with goat milk yogurt mixed in, but was truly a wonder. A cantaloupe explosion in my mouth. I looked over at Josh after we got the smoothies. He was holding the cup gently and affectionately in both hands, staring into it like he had finally found the love of his life. He didn't utter a word as he stared into the cup for what had to have been 10 or 15 minutes, while breaking his adoring gaze only to take slow, lingering sips and nod his head in silent approval after each one. Every time we get together to this day, Josh and I talk about those cantaloupe smoothies.

    The younger guy who worked there offered us a ride to a hotel up the road a couple of miles, which we accepted. We did not plan on paying for a room, as Josh was intent on convincing the operator of the hotel to let us stay for free somehow. He tried this and it did not work, but the lady at the hotel said we could camp next to the building, come in for the continental breakfast in the morning, and even use the outdoor pool. We could do all of this as long as we abided by two conditions. She said, "There's two rules — no swimming naked in the pool and no pissin' in the direction of the hotel when you're camped out there." We told her that her rules seemed reasonable enough.

    Josh and I swam and let out shouts of joy as we splashed around in the pool, then drank the beer the lady at the desk had recommended to us, which was called Polygamy Porter (Slogan: Why Have Just One?), until the sun started to set. We then put our tents up and made a small campfire. Josh played his ukulele and sang while we cooked JiffyPop on the fire's leaping flames. Dinner was eaten in the firelight. I had my usual ravioli in a can, but Josh got more creative. He made some ramen noodles, then began adding chunks of Spam and pita bread into the mix. He called it Spamen with dumplings.

The next day, we walked into Capitol Reef National Park. Once again, we went from walking through barren, lifeless desert to exploring fertile groves of orchards, trees covered in green leaves, and wildlife. All of this was nestled in amongst grand buttes and mesas along the Fremont River. We saw petroglyphs from natives who had settled in the area some 1,000 years before. Deer ran across the road constantly. We went into an apple orchard along the road and ate several apples. You couldn't carry any out, but you could eat as many as you wanted while within the orchard fencing for free. We took a couple for the road anyway. The gurgling Fremont lured us in. We dunked our heads into the river's clear current.

Josh and I were both in no particular hurry, and we acted like it. We took breaks often and enjoyed our surroundings slowly. One afternoon, we stopped and both took naps in the middle of a pasture. Raindrops hitting our faces woke us up after some time. Josh often walked ahead of me when we were on the move. He spent much of this time as our mini-pack leader performing spectacular displays of air guitar and imaginary drum solos. I noticed drivers on the road watching him and laughing as he flopped around and switched from instrument to instrument without an ounce of shame.

Josh became increasingly adamant about locating and eating a prickly pear cactus, so I encouraged him to do so. It did not take us long to find one that he apparently thought looked tasty. Josh immediately set about trying to remove the cactus' slimy green flesh from underneath its heavily fortified outer skin, which was covered in razor sharp points. He screamed out in pain every few seconds while trying to do this, and was soon bleeding from numerous puncture wounds. After a while, the cactus was placed inside Wilson, I suppose for safe keeping until Josh decided to resume his efforts later. When I unpacked Wilson for the last time in San Francisco, however, the cactus was still in there.

    Small town Utah was a hard place to get an understanding of. The people were nice in some places, but very mean in others. I suppose this is true everywhere on the map, but this disparity seemed more obvious there. Some of the more evil looking stare downs I got were in Utah. People seemed outwardly paranoid in a lot of areas. At one gas station, a loaded 12-gauge shotgun sat behind the cash register in plain view. I know it was loaded because I asked the store attendant if it was. People seemed pretty skeptical of Josh and myself. One guy simply would not believe that we had walked to Utah from the east coast. He called our claim a "bullshit story." One day, Josh and I were taking a break under the awning of a closed general store when a guy came up and told us we should leave, simply because he didn't like the look of us. He wasn't even the owner or an employee of the store, just a concerned citizen looking to get rid of the riffraff.

    With all this being said, the people who *were* kind to us were exceptionally helpful and supportive. We scored a free hotel room stay at the Road Creek Lodge in Loa, simply because we asked. A guy pulled over to the side of the road and gave me $1.70 in change one day. He said it was all he had with him, but that he wanted to make sure I got it. Country Dave's, a charming general store and restaurant in the town of Sigurd, advertised their hours as "Mon. - Sun. 5:00 - Dark." Josh and I walked in a bit past dark, but it wasn't a big deal. We still received delicious patty melts and friendly service.

After several more nights camping under the bright Utah sky and sitting around campfires, Josh had to head south. A bit past Sigurd, where Route 24 intersected with Interstate 70, Josh hopped onto the I-70 on-ramp and began hitching his way down to Las Vegas. He then continued to Los Angeles, then north up the California, Oregon, and Washington coasts over the course of the next month or so.

Josh leaving hit me pretty hard, I must admit. I walked a short day into Salina after his departure to look for a place to rest and be sad for a while. I knew there was a Burger King there somewhere, so I stopped to ask where it was at a local tourism office. The old curmudgeon inside told me that the "Booger King" was just up the road. I made it to the Booger King and ate five or six burgers over the course of a few hours and drank endless soda refills. I found myself feeling unbearably lonely for the first time in a while. I wished I had tried to convince Josh to just walk all the way to San Francisco with me.

Chapter 20: Savage Of The Desert

    I camped in a town park in the town of Scipio a couple of days after Josh and I parted ways. When I called the local police station to ask permission to do so, the officer said, "I'll have 20 calls the second you start setting up your tent because people have nothing better to do, but go for it." He came by several times during the night to check on me. I talked to Coulson on the phone for a while before I went to sleep. He had spent his day trying to outrun a tornado on foot up in Iowa. He vented to me about that while I did the same about the truck that almost hit me that afternoon. We were talking or exchanging text messages on a nearly daily basis, which helped me maintain some level of sanity, as he was really one of the only people I knew at the moment who could relate to me.
    The next morning, I went to the Texaco station in Scipio to buy a drink and eat breakfast. On one of the gas station's bathroom walls someone had written: "Email ____@yahoo.com for nude pictures of my wife." Another woefully scribed: "We broke down."
    The cashier lady at the gas station told me all about her life. She said that she hated working there and that she made $4,000 a month online in some pyramid scheme, but couldn't quit because she was the only employee left. She asked where I was going, so I told her. She asked, "You're takin' 50 across Nevada?" I said I most definitely was.
    "Ooowee, that will be one hell of a time," she said with a laugh.
    "Should be fun."
    "What are you gonna do about all them mountains?"
    "What do you mean?"

"Honey, go over there and look at that map near the door, the topographic one," she instructed.

I walked over to the large map by the door and got a sinking feeling in my stomach the second I saw it. I had honestly thought Nevada was mostly flat. It was not. There were dozens of north-to-south mountain ranges running through the middle of the state, right where I would be walking. Big ones, too. I'd known there would be *some* mountains, but had never realized that Nevada was actually the most mountainous state in the lower 48 states. This is a fitting illustration of just how unprepared I was nearly all of the time. I didn't plan ahead much, mainly because if I thought any further than the present day, I was liable to go out of my mind due to the sheer magnitude of the task at hand. I hardly ever thought about San Francisco, let alone what lied ahead in Nevada.

I looked at the cashier lady and said, "That's a lot of mountains."

~

My route took me on an Interstate 15 frontage road for a while, where I walked along with muscular bulls as they foraged around for food. It was open range. They stomped around and seemed like they did not enjoy my presence, which made me uneasy. A farmer let me camp next to his corn field for the night about 15 miles from Delta, my last civilized stop before entering Nevada. I smoked a cigar and watched the darkness come in silence.

I was anxious to get to Delta. I had a mail drop there full of goodies from one of my grandparents back home, as well as a package containing my ukulele, which I'd asked my mom to ship to me from Maine. Early on during my walk to Delta, I found a Millard County first place ribbon from the county fair on the side of the road and gave it to Wilson as a small token of my appreciation for all of his service, complete with a small speech and roadside pinning ceremony.

Not long after leaving Delta, I made it to Hinckley, a town with nearly nothing in it, then began a stretch of 83 lonesome miles to the Nevada border. In the early afternoon, a car pulled over onto the side of the road ahead, and a lady hopped out of it and approached me. She introduced herself as Jean. She was driving across America with her dog, Libby. Jean had driven by me just a few minutes earlier and couldn't quite understand why I was out there in the middle of the desolation all alone with a baby stroller. Her curiosity got the best of her after a couple of miles, so she turned around to come back and see what the deal was. She later wrote this on her website:

"I turned around. And sure enough what I thought I saw was indeed what I did see. A young kid, walking all alone, in the searing Utah sun, pushing one of those baby jogger strollers, (no baby inside) instead, it was loaded with gear. This guy – ALL alone, on one of the most remote stretches of two-lane highway I have witnessed on this trip. Heat of the day, walking out on the highway, in the middle of the desert."

We talked for a while in the whipping Utah wind about all the circumstances that led us to meet in such an unconventional place. The reasons behind Jean's trip were rooted in a certain degree of hardship and uncertainty, much like my own. Our conversation got deep quickly, as they tend to do between travelers who are both searching for something.

Libby made her way out of Jean's car and snuggled right up to me. I knelt down and she sat next to me, then leaned her head into my leg. I envied Jean for having such a sweet road companion. After talking for a while, Jean gave me a long hug and left. For whatever reason, that hug meant a great deal to me. I had never been a big hugger, but it made my day to experience any sort of human connection out there — to feel like I had even the most temporary of allies in the wilderness.

~

I battled a fierce thunder and lightning storm in my tent the following night. Wind slammed against the walls of my home at speeds of at least 40 or 50 miles per hour. The only way to keep the tent upright was to sit and lean back with all my strength against the wall corresponding with whichever way the wind was coming from. I shifted around constantly as the wind changed directions. Lightning cracked as it made contact with the desert floor nearby. The thunder that followed shook the ground.

Despite all of this, I was as happy as a clam at high tide. I yelled at the storm and howled like a wolf as I ate one of the MREs I received in Delta. A small pack of Skittles was my dessert for the evening, so I savored them one by one as I was jolted around by the wind gusts. When the storm eventually died down later in the night, I reflected on everything and decided I was becoming a very odd person out there.

After another day of walking and camping, I found myself on the verge of entering Nevada. I woke up early on my last morning in Utah and watched the sun rise over the desert, while silently taking stock of where I was mentally and physically.

Mentally, I had never been better. I felt relaxed and content with the world and my place in it. Every morning I woke up, I felt like the day ahead was surely going to be the best one of my life. I should have felt lonely, but didn't. It only took a few days after Josh left for me to get back into the swing of things. Adaptability had come to be perhaps my greatest skill. I spent my days singing, taking in the natural beauty that surrounded me everywhere I looked, and talking to Wilson and imaginary people. Sometimes I even got to talk to real people.

Physically, I felt like a machine. I could walk 25 miles in a day and not be tired. That was something. My physical appearance, however, was an entirely different matter. I had a nasty neck beard and other assorted thin, patchy areas of hair on my face. My mustache was toeing the line between funny and creepy. My hair was dried out and coated in dirt. It stood straight up at all times. My bandana was filthy and smelled like what I would imagine blood, sweat, and tears to smell like if they were to be combined. My tan lines were absurd. Certain parts of me were as white as the day I left the beach in Delaware, while others were burned to a crisp after months of slow cooking. I looked like a real-life savage of the desert.

In dirt-crusted socks, I slid my feet into my trusty walking shoes as one last Utah valley lit up ahead in the morning sun. Nevada sat just over the mountains.

Chapter 21: The Loneliest Road

In 1986, *LIFE Magazine* heralded U.S. Route 50 in Nevada as The Loneliest Road In America. The *LIFE* article quoted a representative from AAA, who said, "There are no points of interest. We don't recommend it. We warn all motorists not to drive there unless they're confident of their survival skills."

The Loneliest Road lies in what is known as the Basin And Range Province of the western United States. The road basically just winds up, over, and down 17 jagged mountain ranges and across even more high desert basins. Highway 50 exemplifies the most beautiful sort of monotony. It's desolate enough to make you nervous, but the surrounding scenery is beautiful enough to calm your nerves. It is a wild and unique place where virtually anything goes. And I was going to walk across it alone.

At the Utah/Nevada border I found myself at a place called The Border Inn. It was made up of a small compound of buildings that straddled the state line. Half of the establishment was in Utah, where they sold gasoline at Utah prices, as well as items in a small convenience store. There were motel rooms there too. The other half of the complex was in Nevada, where you could get an inexpensive, satisfying meal at a restaurant, play slot machines, smoke a cigarette in the bar while drinking, carry an unconcealed weapon (not in the bar, however), and enjoy all of your favorite vices in relative peace.

I sat at a small table near the bar on the Nevada side of the building to use the free WiFi, and watched as a few locals, presumably residents of the nearby town of Baker, filed in one by one. They each took a seat at the bar, greeted the bartender, ordered a drink, and lit up a cigarette. Their conversations became increasingly lively as time went on, as they would at any bar.

As I silently watched everything unfold, another man walked in and sat down to join the gang at the bar. The drunkest lady at the bar, a leathery looking woman in her forties with dark black hair, exclaimed, "Welcome to the bar, where the goods are odd and the odds are good!"

A frail old man sat a couple tables over from me. He was talking to his salad as he ate it, just looking straight into it with a deep focus and babbling on and on. With each bite he'd say, "Hmmm, yup, hmmm," and "Yum, mmm, mmm, that's good, yup," and "Ooooh, yeeeah, yum, that's good."

Two young women walked into the room and sat down. They were holding hands, a cute couple. One of them had very short hair and was wearing baggy jeans and a t-shirt. The drunk leathery lady seemed to know her partner and said, "Who's this, your boyfriend?" loudly across the bar. Awkward silence ensued for a few moments, and then the drunk lady realized she was mistaken. She apologized by simply saying, "I'm drunk" with a smile, then took another sip from her drink. I loved everyone in the place.

Paying the cashier in the Utah side of the building for a $5 campsite, I made my way outside to set up my tent in a fierce windstorm that had risen up out of nowhere. Wilson took a few blasts to his side and went up on one wheel, nearly tipping over. Gusts through the valley sometimes topped 100 miles per hour, according to the clerk in the store.

In the morning, I was practically jumping up and down with excitement to get further into Nevada. I left the Border Inn with the same adventurous buzz I carried over each new state line, but knew a serious struggle was ahead. I'd learn a lot in the coming few hundred miles. Ahead there were heart-stopping switchback turns, narrow road shoulders, wild drivers, mountain lions, pelting downpours of rain, freezing night temperatures, 50+ mile per hour winds, hailstorms, rattlesnakes, territorial wild horses, food shortages, and odd local folks. It was going to be one hell of a time.

~

My first major stop in Nevada was in Eureka, which sat 62 miles away from The Border Inn. I would be camping in the basins between the mountain ranges whenever possible during the trip there, mainly for their higher temperatures and less severe weather patterns. Oftentimes this meant camping right out in the open just a handful of yards off the road. The basins typically laid out for 10-20 miles between the mountain ranges and passes, acting as important recovery opportunities for me between the arduous battles brought on by the climbs over the mountains. Most of the terrain was dry, high desert. Interspersed throughout these thirst-inducing stretches were patches of shrubby forests, but shade was usually even at a bare minimum there. Temperatures during the day were high but at night routinely dropped to 30-40 degrees. I struggled up Sacramento Pass (elev. 7,154 ft.) and Connors Pass (elev. 7,722 ft.).

Most of the vehicles on 50 fell into two main categories. The first of these was RVs and campers, and the second was government vehicles of all types — Department of Transportation, Highway Patrol, Bureau of Land Management. Regardless of their category, every vehicle on 50 moved at a tremendous clip. The speed limit on the narrow two-lane road was a generous 70 miles-per-hour, but most of the cars and trucks that passed me cruised along at a steady 85-90. For decades, Nevada did not have a speed limit on rural roads such as Highway 50. As far as I could tell, nothing had really changed. The 70 mile-per-hour figure posted on the road's speed limit signs was nothing more than a formality that was enforced lightly, if at all.

It was on this fast-paced stretch of road that I learned most motorists would rather endanger the life of a fellow human being than drive for roughly two seconds on a rumble strip. The Loneliest Road had one down its centerline along much of its length. Countless times I watched drivers deliberate as they approached me regarding what they should do about the rumble strip predicament. Did they want to narrowly miss me or possibly even make contact, or have to hear that really annoying rumbling sound for a couple of seconds? More often than not, people chose the former. I spent a lot of time thinking about how strange humans are out there. At least a couple dozen cars and trucks forced me to jump into the roadside ditch to avoid being hit as they came at me, even though the road was perfectly straight and there was rarely so much as a single other car within 20 or 30 miles.

~

I finally arrived in Ely, one of the most well known historical towns in Nevada, and got a room at the posh Four Sevens Motel. The ancient sign in front of it advertised it as "NEW!" My suite cost $35 a night and sat just a few blocks from several casinos and the local brothel. Location, location, location.

I chose not to contribute to the local economy by partaking in any of its signature vices during my first night in town, instead opting to drink a six-pack of Budweiser and watch TV in my room with Wilson. The next morning, I made the decision to stick around for another day and night. Despite the array of suspicious stains on the carpet in my room, the place was such a bargain that I couldn't resist.

I visited the White Pine Public Museum in downtown Ely during my day off, which was a wonderful establishment. It was full of all sorts of goodies such as old Coke machines, railroad cars, a 100+ year old school house, a fully intact jail cell, military uniforms, the bones of a giant prehistoric cave bear found in a local mine, fossilized dinosaur footprints, and my personal favorite, a petrified human foot. The foot, still in its original leather shoe, was found in a local mine. Henry, the welcoming and insightful museum curator, said as we bent over to examine the severed foot more closely, "It's either the foot of a dead miner or something that an animal dug up from a cemetery and hauled into the mine shaft. You can see the bone in there if you look closely."

After learning a lot about the area's history and making several trips back to the case that held the human foot, I made my way back toward the motel, stopping at the Economy Drug & Old Fashioned Fountain on the way. A milkshake sounded good.

While in high school, I mentioned to my mom that I thought a girl at school was pretty, to which she replied, "Why don't you ask her out for a soda?" I laughed and responded, "Mom, this isn't the fifties, I'm not just going to take her down to the malt shop." My brother and I had always laughed at her about that suggestion. It's been a long-standing family joke since.

Good thing my mom has a sense of humor. I thought about this as I saw the sign for the Old Fashioned Fountain on Aultman Street in downtown Ely, and knew I had to find out why my mom had thought such a place would be a fitting venue for a first date.

The place ended up being perfect. Pictures of Elvis and Marilyn Monroe lined the walls, along with a collection of dusty 45s. Round chrome bar stools with bright red seats sat in front of a polished black countertop, which sat atop a black and white checkered floor. And to bring the whole thing home, it wasn't some dumbass high school kid with an attitude making my milkshake. The lady putting it together fit the look I imagined an old fashioned fountain operator would have to a tee. She had a mound of hair that was puffed up so big that it made her face look strangely small. She wore deep red lipstick. Her cheeks were rosy with a generous layer of blush. She was a machine behind the counter, a whirl of movement producing milkshakes and soda floats that seemed to formulate out of thin air in seconds. She called everyone "hun."

The milkshake was thick, sugary, and delicious. I felt a sense of nostalgia, even though the dream I was living in there for a few moments was modeled after a time I had never experienced personally. I could finally understand my mom's reasoning behind her suggestion for that date. I silently toasted to her and my high school sweetheart that never was. I definitely would have taken her there had I grown up in Ely and/or I had lived during the 1950s.

~

I had mixed feelings about Ely. It had a sort of off-putting vibe, like it was trying too hard to be a miniature version of Las Vegas or Reno. Many people I ran into cited the same reason for not liking it. Walking out of the west side of town, a lone hitchhiker sat on the other side of the road. He was filthy and had a big beard. I said, "Where are you heading, man?"

He replied, "Just tryin' to get the fuck outta here."

~

My next destination, aside from a few days' worth of dusty roadside break spots and campsites, was Eureka, which sat 78 miles west of Ely. I walked over four passes during those 78 miles — Robinson, Little Antelope, Pancake, and Pinto, and camped in the basins between each of them at night. The backdrops to some of my camping locations over those few days were stunning to the point that they almost looked fake, like if I threw a rock as hard as I could, it would fly through the canvases they were painted on. The afternoons stayed hot, but things continued to cool off considerably during the early morning and evening hours. The sun illuminated everything in a way that seemed impossibly bright — the brown desert sand, the green sage and creosote bushes, and endless golden patches of grass and scattered chaparral.

A strange visitor came to my tent the night before I made it to Eureka. I woke up suddenly around midnight to the sound of feet stomping around just a few feet away. The steps were much too heavy to be human. I yelled, "Hey! Get out of here!" and slammed my hand into the side of my tent to get rid of the intruder. In reply I received a powerful neigh from the visitor, a wild horse.

More wild horses live in Nevada than all of the other states in the U.S. combined. A cattle fence, which was just a couple of feet from my face, was the only barrier between my new horse friend and myself. I had actually bungeed my tent's rainfly directly to the fence instead of using a tent stake. The horse continued to pace back and forth just a few feet from my home for the remainder of the night.

    The sky was full of dark clouds when I awoke in the morning. I rushed to get my gear packed into Wilson and beat the fast approaching rain. Packed up just in time, I got my umbrella out and plopped down on the ground underneath it. Raindrops bounced off it steadily as I ate breakfast. There was a short, isolated tree about 50 yards away. Under it stood the previous night's intruder. It was his version of an umbrella. I yelled, "This is bullshit, right?" but received no response. We stared at one another for a while, and then the rain stopped.

    I battled with Pinto Summit that morning. The rain picked up again as I began my ascent. With each minute that it continued to not let up, my energy dwindled. The road was steep. Rainwater poured down the pavement like a river, making it difficult to push an 80 pound Wilson against the current. Within sight of the summit, my body nearly gave out. I staggered to the front of Wilson, opened him up, grabbed my jar of peanut butter, and forced three heaping spoonfuls into my mouth one at a time. Thankfully, the calorie boost this provided got me though. My entire body was shivering uncontrollably as I reached the top. Just as I made it to a pull-off at the summit, the clouds cleared, the rain stopped, and the sun emerged. I removed as much clothing as I could and sat out to dry in the warm, glorious rays. I guzzled a soda as I smiled at my good fortune, choosing to ignore the horrible walk that had gotten me to that point. The guardrail next to me had "ALTITUDE SICKNESS" spray-painted on it.

After easing my way down Pinto, I finally arrived in Eureka and called the host I had arranged there ahead of time with the help of a friend. A sign read: You Are Entering The Friendliest Town On The Loneliest Road In America.

Chapter 22: Basin And Range

My host's name was Barbie. Barbie hadn't always lived in Eureka, but she was as much of a local as anyone there. She knew the town's history inside and out, all the local goings-on and gossip, and loved the place to death. She lived in a charming old house just a couple of blocks off Main Street. The house was full of antiques, a range of oddities she had collected over a span of several decades. A mint condition, baby blue 1950s outdoor grill sat on the front porch. It had never been used. On two sides of the house, massive 100-year-old Poplar trees had grown so tall and wide that they pushed the outside edges of the porch upward.

Barbie took me out on the town to celebrate my first night in Eureka. Our first stop was The Keyhole Bar. Housed in a skinny building squished between two large brick buildings, one of them being the old Eureka opera house, it would be easy to walk right on by the place if you didn't already know it was there.

We both took seats at the bar. The ceiling was covered with sheets of tin metal roofing. The wooden beams that jutted out from between the roofing sheets were coated with money. Bills of all denominations were pinned, glued, and taped on every square inch of available space. The walls were plastered with bumper stickers, along with Jack Daniels, Coors, and Budweiser memorabilia. Behind us sat a line of slot machines and a cigarette vending machine.

The people in The Keyhole were especially friendly to me because I had come in with Barbie. It was always good to have an "in" at these types of places. A lady came up to talk to us, commented on my supposed good looks, and put her arm around me. She held the embrace for a couple of minutes until she was done talking with Barbie. Friendliest Town on the Loneliest Road, indeed. The beer at The Keyhole was cold and refreshing, and its ambiance was relaxed. I instantly knew I'd be one of its regular patrons if I ever were to settle down in Eureka. It also proved to be an affordable destination, as Barbie had free drink tokens to every bar in town.

From the Keyhole we moved a bit further down Main Street to the Owl Club. The main attraction there, at least to me, was the local folks who frequented the place. I spent a lot of time talking to them, many of whom were workers in a nearby mine. One of the more colorful characters there was an older hippie looking guy. He was tall, had long gray hair, and was wearing a black bandana. Every minute or so, his thunderous laugh roared across the entire bar. Nearly everyone at the bar was smoking, and my eyes quickly dried out as a result. With eyes as dry as the surrounding desert, I saw the old hippie take a drag off his cigarette that was so long that a quarter of it burned back before he exhaled. I talked with everyone I could and was thankful they took the time to talk back. I was exhausted from over 20 miles of walking, filthy because I still hadn't showered yet, bleary eyed from the smoke, and slightly drunk, but couldn't have been more pleased.

The only disturbing thing about The Owl Club was the enormous stuffed mountain lion on display directly behind the bar. When she noticed me staring at it, Barbie filled me in on just how large the local mountain lion population was. It was so large, in fact, that hunters were paid a bounty for getting rid of them. Every Eureka local had at least one mountain lion story. Whether a dog or cat of theirs had been killed by one, they had shot one themselves, or they had seen one walking right through town, they all had tales of the killer felines. Not long before I arrived in town, one especially pesky lion had eaten a local judge's cat, as well as stolen the steaks that the county sheriff had set out next to his grill in his back yard. The killer/thief was gunned down right in downtown Eureka the day after its little crime spree.

For as scary as that story was, another I heard got to me even more. It was about someone who had been riding their horse across America over the previous summer. Their horse was killed right off Highway 50 near Eureka in a mountain lion attack. The beast pounced from some roadside brush cover right onto the horse's head and neck. I sent a text message to Coulson, telling him about the person's horse being attacked and killed right on the side of the road.

His reply: "You're next."

~

I ended up taking two full days off in Eureka. When I wasn't hanging out with Barbie, I walked around the town's historic downtown area and explored as much as possible.

Eureka had an interesting past. The town suffered major fire damage in 1879 after most of it went up in flames. This caused residents to rebuild many of the buildings with brick. Two of these beautiful brick buildings, the opera house and courthouse, were on the list of things I had to see while there. The courthouse still retained its original decadence with its chandeliers and pressed tin ceiling. It is the one building visitors to Eureka are likely to notice first upon arriving there. The opera house, which sat nearby, was an elegant brick building with skinny white columns holding up an outdoor second-story balcony. Inside the opera house there was a carefully restored auditorium with balcony seating, polished wooden floors, and a detailed painted backdrop behind the stage that looked exactly as it would have in the late 1800s, complete with local advertisements from the period. Since its construction was completed in 1880, the opera house had accommodated crowds for operas, dances, concerts, and both silent and talking movies.

In addition to these important buildings, Eureka also has the only five-hole outhouse in the state of Nevada, which sits proudly on Main Street. According to the sign next to it, "The outhouse itself has had a troubled past. It has been moved numerous times and has been the center of a legal dispute." The outhouse was a good indicator of just how lonely it could get out there. A person will take some company wherever they can find it in lonesome basin and range territory.

Barbie took me on a tour of the largely forgotten, decrepit cemeteries just outside of town. Cracked and crumbling wooden and stone grave markers were scattered across the cemetery lots' dry gravel. Rusted iron gates stood as remnants of once well guarded and maintained graves. All clues as to where the paths between the rows of grave plots once were had vanished. They had been eroded and blown away over the years. I didn't know who lied under each footstep as I walked around. We spent at least an hour reading the worn epitaphs on the grave markers, while trying to distinguish the dates on them as well as we could. The oldest date of death I could make out was 1824. I'd heard of ghost towns, but didn't think I'd ever visit a ghost cemetery — a place where so many rested, yet were completely forgotten and lost in time.

As we drove back to Barbie's house after the cemetery visit, I thought about just how much I loved Eureka. It was easy to enjoy wandering down its clean streets and visiting the dozens of points of interest scattered among them. The people I met were friendly and welcoming. There was a strong sense of community that reached all the way across town. I learned the local police would gladly pick up any elderly person who needed a ride somewhere. They would also provide a free ride home from the bar should someone have too much to drink and ask for it. Every single person I met in Eureka looked me straight in the eye when we spoke. There was no false sense of superiority among any of its residents that I encountered. They looked at me like a person, like a human being, not some dumb kid who was just trying to escape the real world. I knew that look all to well by the time I arrived in Eureka. My survival depended on reading people in an instant, and I instantly felt at home in that weird little town. Mainly, I just think it was nice to be around people who really seemed to care about one another, and even me. The rest of the world could learn a lot from Eureka, Nevada.

~

Austin was my next stop and sat 60 miles to the west. I once again trudged into the high desert toward yet another mountain range that needed crossing. On the way to Austin, I encountered my first Loneliest Road construction project. The workers I met at these construction zones were entertaining, to say the least. They not only had to do their assigned work, but many of them also took on the role of entertainer for the agitated motorists who were forced to wait up to 30 minutes or more for their chances to pass through the work zones. The flaggers at each end of these work zones were definitely the most intriguing characters of the working crews.

Walking up to the first flagger I met, I said hello. "Hey buddy, want a cold drink? I got water, Gatorade, beer in that cooler in the back of the car, help yourself!" he said.

"Gatorade would be awesome," I said. I had to dig through the cooler for a bit to find something that wasn't a can of Natural Ice, which my flagger friend was drinking during the lulls in traffic.

"Where ya headed?" he asked.

"San Francisco. I'm walking across the U.S."

"No way, you ever get any pussy?"

Being accustomed to answering that question by then, I laughed and said no.

"They must not like that you're walkin' I guess. Well, buddy, I'll tell ya what. If you head into San Francisco from the north, you'll be goin' through Marin County. All the pussy in the world there. It's where I grew up. And the women got money, too!" he said. I said I'd keep that nugget of information in mind. For the next two days he stopped and said hi to me on his ride to and from work. He offered me a beer each time.

At another roadwork area, a female construction worker blew bubbles through a big, circular wand at passing motorists as they finally escaped their 20-minute delay. This simple act worked wonders. Scowls turned to smiles as each car passed her. Everybody loves bubbles.

The further toward the center of Nevada I got, the more hazardous the roads became. A car missed hitting me by a couple feet or less at least twice a day. After one particularly close call, I was seething with anger. As I was swearing and throwing an all around fit on the

Life On Foot 223

side of the road, a car came up from behind and stopped in the road next to me. I shot the driver an angry look. I hated him instinctively.

He yelled, "Are you that walker dude?" out his halfway rolled down window.

"I think so."

"Kick ass!" he screamed as he threw a $20 bill out the window before speeding off. I picked the bill up off the warm pavement, waved as the car disappeared around a corner, and was surprised to find myself in forgiving mood.

~

The terrain through the basins was dry, yet full of color. Blue skies appeared for most mornings and evenings, and it rained every day like clockwork during the middle hours of the afternoon. I'd begin watching a storm roll across whatever basin I was in around noon each day. At around 2 or 3 PM, I'd be huddled under my umbrella waiting for it to pass over.

I walked at length along the old Pony Express Trail, the pathway utilized by the revolutionary rapid mail service that offered people the fastest way of communication at the time from 1860 to 1861. The Pony Express advertised that it could deliver a letter from St. Joseph, Missouri to San Francisco, California in just ten days, in essentially the greatest relay race on Earth. Along with the old Pony Express route, the Lincoln Highway also joined up with the Loneliest Road. The Lincoln Highway, made official in 1913, was one of the original cross-country routes for motorists in America. It ran from New York City to San Francisco. Known as the "Main Street Across America," it brought commerce and vibrant prosperity to many small towns and cities along the route, and did much to promote the concept of constructing more long-haul driving routes in the U.S.

As I approached the town of Austin, I collided with Austin Summit, a 7,484 foot monster I'd been hearing warnings about for some time. It turned out to be not as bad as I expected. I reached the top of Austin Pass in the early afternoon. Ecstatic, as I thought I had just conquered the pass that everyone had been warning me about, I decided to take a nice long break as a reward. I talked to a few friends on the phone, ate a larger-than-normal lunch, and did some journaling. Deciding to make the final little push into Austin about an hour and a half after beginning this leisurely break, I crested the final 100 yards or so of the supposed summit and was greeted with a demoralizing view.

The road ahead led into a steep decline, which was then followed by a stretch of switchbacks leading up to the *actual* summit. I had been sadly mistaken. The journey to the top of Austin Summit was really just beginning.

I struggled up the narrow road and felt frustrated at first, but the fact that such a dumb mistake had caused me to waste a good portion of the day actually ended up helping my cause. Taking that long break had been such an idiotic move that I had no choice but to laugh about it. Finally crossing over the summit and dripping with sweat, I was greeted with a splendid view — my reward for topping the Toiyabe Range. The air was crisp and clear. I could smell a rainstorm coming my way. The town of Austin sat quietly on the edge of the valley below, which was technically still part of the west side of the Toiyabes. A golden basin stretched out toward the next mountain range I'd have to walk over. The road between the top of the pass and Austin displayed the most bizarre switchbacks I'd seen since being on Highway 50 back in West Virginia. Walking in a straight line toward Austin, I could have been there in minutes, but the actual distance to town was increased at least fivefold by the curves in the road.

As I began my descent down the pass, something hit the brim of my hat with a thud. Then it happened again. And again. I thought one of the many ravens that had been circling me for most of the day had finally hit its target. Then it happened again. And again.

Hail? Seriously? Marble-sized balls of ice came down more furiously with each passing second. I got my umbrella out and took cover underneath it as hailstones pelted it and crunched beneath my feet. I steered Wilson with one hand while holding my umbrella shelter with the other. The hail finally let up as I got into town, but only managed to transform itself into to cold, driving rain. I definitely preferred the hail.

My first impression of Austin was that it had to be an old mining town, which proved to be correct. Most of the buildings were constructed of brick, many of which had exposed and crumbling sections. Where Eureka had done so much reconditioning, Austin seemed to have just let things be how they were. It was endearing nonetheless.

After silver was discovered near Austin in 1862, the town exploded in population. Over 10,000 people called it home during its heyday. The economic boom proved to be short lived, however, and most of those people had moved on to other places and newer mining rushes by 1867. The version of Austin I was seeing had a population of a little over 300 people, and the town claimed to be a "living ghost town."

I wound up getting a motel room in Austin, settling on the Pony Express Motel as a suitable place to get some rest. I had checked out one other motel in town before getting to The Pony Express, but the lady at its front desk told me the cost for their rooms was "probably more than I could pay" after seeing me come in the door. She was rude, but probably right.

There was a bar in town that advertised an upcoming event centered around "Serbian Christmas." It looked like the kind of place I would like. I could imagine the friendly owners inside (Serbian, of course) and a bunch of locals kicking back and having a few drinks. I wanted to join them so badly. I usually only got to go to places like that when someone took me, as my budget didn't tend to have much wiggle room to work with. This bummed me out as I thought about all the Serbian friends I could be making. I didn't know any Serbians. But it was either the hotel or the bar, and I really needed a shower after a few days of hiking in the high desert and the afternoon's hailstorm and rain.

I decided I'd have to come back to Austin sometime to see a different side of things. Surely someday I would have enough money to explore the town's various interesting looking establishments more thoroughly as paying customer. At the very least, I'd be back to see what Serbian Christmas was all about.

Stocked up on food and water and ready to go the following morning, rain started coming down right on cue as I walked out of Austin. Right on the edge of town, I heard a voice yelling in the distance. I turned around to see my beer drinking flagger friend waving from afar. He must have lived in Austin. He yelled, "Good luck, man!" from the porch of the local laundromat. I waved back at him. What a great guy.

Chapter 23: It's Like This Place, But Not As Nice

The sun disappeared and clouds rolled in as I descended into the basin in front of me. The clouds blanketed the mountains all around. The rain they brought with them drizzled down persistently for my first 15 miles of walking out of Austin. Between my location in the desolate basin and Fallon, my next major stop, there were two gas station/bar/motel/campground stops I could rest up at — Cold Springs and Middlegate Station. Crossing over the Desatoya Mountains and New Pass Summit, I got to Cold Springs first.

Arriving in the early evening, I went inside the building, paid for a camping spot, and splurged on a barbeque chicken dinner with a beer. As I did this, it struck me as odd that I had gotten so frustrated just a couple of days earlier about not getting to go to the Serbian bar in Austin because of money issues. *That* was out of the question, but a chicken dinner and a beer at Cold Springs was just fine. I didn't feel bad about it at all as I handed over my debit card to buy a full meal when Wilson was already packed with food, but a beer in Austin would have sent me right over the edge. It made no sense. It seemed almost as if I made up dramatic events and dilemmas in my head whenever I felt I needed them. Like whenever the walking seemed too easy and convenient, I needed something else to challenge me, no matter how stupid and nonsensical it was.

I was the only person in the dining area of the bar, so I had plenty of time to think about my flawed reasoning. The waitress in charge of my table was nice enough to talk to me though, and she keep me company for some time. Cold Springs was spotless and looked like it had recently been remodeled. It had a modern and open layout, which strangely, I wasn't too fond of. I was out on the Loneliest Road to see quirky, dirty places. But the barbeque chicken was good, and the beer was refreshing. I was glad I had stopped. All it took was one beer and I was inebriated. That's what long-term dehydration does to you.

As I was wrapping up with dinner, I asked my waitress about Middlegate Station, which was ahead just 15 miles. I'd be there the next day. She said, "It's like this place, but not as nice." It sounded wonderful.

~

In the early afternoon the following day, I came across the landmark that lets a traveler know they are close to Middlegate. It was the famous Shoe Tree, located near mile marker 70 on The Loneliest Road.

The Shoe Tree was exactly what its name implied. It was a bristly cottonwood tree covered in old shoes, which people had thrown up onto it over the years. Most of the people I asked about it said the first shoes were added to the tree sometime in the 1980s. There were work boots, cowboy boots, sandals, dress shoes, athletic sneakers, and high heels dangling from its branches. Unfortunately, someone had taken the liberty to cut down to the original Shoe Tree over the previous winter with a chainsaw. It lied in a ditch next to its original location. The falling of the famous Shoe Tree was a scandal that made news headlines all over Nevada.

I walked up to the ditch to check out the legendary fallen cottonwood. Sections of it were spread out over a wide area. Many hundreds of shoes and boots littered the ground. I could smell the faint yet unmistakable odor of used footwear radiating up from the deep ditch. Someone had constructed a wooden cross in front of the ditch to memorialize the tree. People had written and carved heartfelt messages all over the cross. The most prominent message on it read: SHOE TREE LIVES ON IN OUR SOLES.

Just down the ditch from where the original Shoe Tree rested, a similarly sized cottonwood was beginning to build a substantial shoe collection of its own. It was the New Shoe Tree. It had quite a ways to go, but was doing its best to fill the shoes of its beloved predecessor.

I could see Middlegate from the Shoe Tree and made my way there. It was a ramshackle spread of weathered wooden buildings, which all appeared to be made of salvaged scrap wood. The beams supporting the covered front porch on the main building, which poked up out of a patch of lush trees and bushes, still had bark attached to them and curved slightly. The structure's faded tarpaper roof gleaned white in the beating sun. A horse drawn carriage sat parked against one side of the building next to a few modern-day vehicles. Like any good Wild West saloon, there were horse hitching posts available out front. One of the other buildings in the complex was a long, one-story building that contained motel rooms. An ancient covered wagon (minus the cover) sat in the compacted gravel parking lot, looking like it had been left there during a different century. Behind the main building were assorted trailers and RVs, the homes of those who lived at Middlegate full-time. A generator buzzed in the distance, which powered everything from the appliances in the RVs to the motel lights to the refrigerators inside the bar. It was an off-the-grid paradise.

I walked slowly toward Middlegate's bar/restaurant entrance. A sign read: Welcome To Middlegate - The Middle Of Nowhere. Walking into the bar/restaurant, I saw a long bar and scattered tables, a pool table, a juke box, and so many miscellaneous wall-hung trinkets, photographs, paintings, saddles, and animal horns that I struggled to focus on observing any one of them for any time. The ceiling above all of this was blanketed in money. Bills were taped to the ceiling anywhere that there was room and some places where there wasn't. I approached the bar and took a seat. I'd been told the burgers were good at Middlegate, so I decided to order one.

A raspy voiced old man in a cowboy hat came over to where I was seated, handed me a fly swatter, and said, "Here's your weapon." Everyone was to pull their own weight in the never-ending battle against the bar flies. He took my order for a burger and Coke and told it to the young cook behind the bar.

I took a look around. Behind the bar there was an impressive collection of bumper stickers — "I Love Animals, They're Delicious" and "God Bless Our Troops, Especially Our Snipers" were a couple that stood out. Several other travelers sat at a table behind me, as well as two military guys, presumably from the naval air station in Fallon. One was in full uniform and the other was not, but he was wearing military boots.

The old man behind the bar chain smoked cigarettes and sipped on a can of Milwaukee's Best as he talked to me. I asked about mountain lions, and he said they weren't as much of a problem around there as they were in the eastern part of the state. He said, "We have these big lizards that come out every year, and we get an owl every *two* years."

My burger appeared in front of me shortly. It was the best burger I had ever tasted, no question. It was so good that it almost made me angry. I felt bitter about the fact that I could not eat one or more of them every day for the rest of my life without having to move all the way out to Middlegate. Finishing it quickly, I contemplated getting a second one, but decided I'd better move on. There was still a lot of walking to do for the day, and lugging around one burger in my stomach was going to be tough enough.

After walking out onto the covered porch, I ended up striking up a conversation with the two military guys I had seen inside. They were taking a break from their work for the day, which was supervising some training exercises out on one of the bombing and gunnery ranges just off Highway 50. One of them, Scott, was still on active duty. The other, Andy, was technically retired from the military, but still worked on the base in Fallon doing specialized training. They were both Navy SEALs. I had never met a SEAL before, let alone two of them at the same time.

After we had talked for a while, Andy said, "When you get to Fallon, give me a call. You're welcome to camp out at my place." He wrote his phone number down in my notebook, and I promised I would call. Feeling beyond excited that I would get to spend some time getting to know a couple of SEALs in Fallon, I hoped the 46 miles between Middlegate and there would pass quickly.

The terrain flattened out quite a bit after Middlegate. Miles accumulated under my feet with ease. Many of the mountains I saw from the road were unbelievably barren, lifeless, and ugly. They looked like tall, hardened sand dunes from another universe. The landscape became more stale by the second, just a baked and sun cracked expanse, devoid of any real benefit other than providing those who dared to explore it with the solitude they must have come for.

~

Making it through the highly exposed flatness just as the sun was making its way below the horizon, I found the first concealment that presented itself as a resting spot, a bunch of low shrubs, and set up camp for the night. Huddling behind the shrubs on the edge of the expansive salt flat that extended limitlessly in almost every direction, I ate some ravioli straight out of the can (AKA, the usual). The sun dipped out of sight, signaling the end of yet another rewarding day.

Not long after dark and as I was beginning to fall asleep, a thunderous noise that was rapidly advancing on my camp shot me to life. I unzipped my tent and stuck my head out of it just in time to see two UH-60 military helicopters fly low overhead. A pair of machine gun barrels poked out of their open side doors as they flew over.

Over the previous few days I had been hearing and seeing a lot of helicopters and fighter jets. The jets typically flew too fast and high for me to spot, but every once in a while they passed through the basins at what couldn't have been more than 300 or 400 feet off the ground. They were deafeningly loud and a marvel to watch. I could also hear the faint popping of machine gun fire coming from the nearby training ranges on most nights. Fighter jets ran training missions and shot off flares in the night sky above. It was a unique fireworks display to complement the already glowing moon and stars. I often found expired 50-millimeter

Life On Foot 233

shell casings right on the side of the road. It felt like I was walking through an active war zone.

I made it to Fallon a couple days after leaving Middlegate. Just outside of town, I stopped at Grimes Point, an archaeological site on the edge of what used to be Lake Lahontan, an Ice Age lake that had since dried up and created much of the salt flat environment I had been walking through. Grimes Point had a trail that lead through a display of hundreds of rocks and boulders that had been decorated with petroglyphs drawn by natives some 6,000 years in the past. I ran my fingers over the 6,000 year old handmade grooves while watching 50 million dollar fighter jets take off from the nearby base. Humans had come far. So had I, I thought.

Chapter 24: On The Range

I called Andy, one of the SEALs I met at Middlegate, and he gave me his address. Little yellow butterflies swarmed me as I walked the short distance to his house.

I got to the house, found Andy sitting outside, and thanked him for his hospitality. I said I was basically just looking for a place to set up my tent for the night and that I'd be heading out in the morning. I never wanted to impose on people's lives more than I had to. He said, "That's fine, but you're welcome to stay a few days if you want. Scott (the other SEAL) is throwing a party over at his place on Saturday (it was Thursday), and I'm sure he'd be glad to have you." After saying that I'd definitely think about it, we sat in the shade under a tall tree near the horse pen where Andy's two horses were galloping around. Wanting to pry every little detail out of him about being a SEAL and all the missions he had been on, I struggled to hold back from blurting out a stream of questions.

Andy had been a SEAL sniper and was currently working in some training programs for prospective SEALs at the base, among others. The base, I found out, was not only home to certain SEALs in training because of its remote location and surrounding mountainous terrain, but was actually better known for being where the U.S. Navy's TOPGUN training school is located. That explained why I had been seeing so many fighter jets on training missions.

Andy ushered me over to his garage, where he showed me his M1 Garand collection. Many of them he had built himself. The iconic M1 was used in three American wars and was the first semi-automatic rifle issued to any armed forces in the world. I shouldered a few of them to get a little taste of history. Andy must have noticed my intense interest in anything he had going on, so he said, "I'll tell you what, Scott and I are supposed to go out to the range tonight and supervise a drill that one of our guys needs to do for a certification. Not the most exciting stuff in the world, just marking targets with some infrared from a helicopter. If you want to, I'll see if you can join us."

"That might not sound exciting to you, but you do realize I've never seen someone mark targets with infrared from a helicopter before, right? I would love to see that," I said back.

He laughed and said, "Alright, let me see what I can do." Andy made a couple of phone calls, after which I was told I would be all set to join he and Scott at the range.

While waiting for the time to come when we would head out to the range, I tried to solve the biggest mystery of the day. While walking outside of Fallon, a small, tan journal sitting a few feet off the road had caught my eye. I picked it up and skimmed through its pages while looking for any clues as to whom it may have belonged to. There were only two clues I managed to find. First, that the owner of the journal was a bicyclist on a cross country trip and traveling west to east, and that their trip had begun in San Francisco. Second, that its owner had been a U.S. Marine at one point in time.

I instantly thought of Mike, the Marine I'd camped with in the baseball dugout back in Colorado. He was heading west and had started his trip in San Francisco. Considering the amount of bicyclists that followed the same route as Mike, I thought the chances of the journal actually being his were still slim. The timing for when I had met him and the dates on the journal entries did match up roughly, however, so there was a chance. The good news was that we had kept in touch. I still had his phone number, so I sent him a text: "Hey man, any chance you lost a tan journal in Nevada? In Fallon and found one, it says that it belonged to a Marine."

A minute later I received a reply: "No fucking way. Yeah I did."

After getting on the phone and confirming the journal was indeed his, we were amazed at how miniscule the chances were of someone finding it at all, let alone that person knowing its owner. The journal had been sitting untouched and buried in the dirt for three months on the side of one of the most remote roads in the country, and the straggler who found it just happened to know the straggler who lost it. I may go through the entire rest of my life without experiencing another coincidence as wild as that one.

~

Scott came to Andy's to pick me up later in the afternoon, as Andy had already gone to the range to set up a few things. I was excited just to see the range, let alone see a helicopter and how the infrared worked.

We went through a high and intimidating metal gate covered in an assortment of strict warning signs against entering without proper clearances, and entered the range. There were a few buildings scattered around, along with old cars, trucks, and a bus, which were all used at targets during training exercises. A mock Soviet missile launcher with fake missiles on it sat alongside the road that led deep into the range. After parking, Andy, Scott, and the soldier who was being tested set up a few pieces of complicated looking equipment.

Everything was set up quickly, and then the waiting began. A bad storm rolled over the mountain range behind us and came swooping through the valley. The wind picked up significantly and turned our surroundings into a whirling sandstorm. Waiting it out in the trucks, we got word from the base that the helicopter had been grounded. We would have to wait until things cleared up to proceed.

The weather cleared after half an hour or so, and we made our way back out to the bench where the equipment was set up. My best observation of how things worked was this: A machine with an invisible infrared laser would shoot a line out to where a chosen target was. The target would not know they were marked, as the laser could not be seen with the naked eye. The only people who could see the laser target would be the people wearing the goggles that picked up its specific frequency of light.

We all sat on a small set of bleachers and waited. Then we waited some more. Scott, Andy and the Marine being tested talked about all kinds of things I didn't understand. They used military terminology and spoke of past deployments. It was fun to just sit there and listen to them.

Eventually we got word from the base that the helicopter wouldn't be sent out. The weather was getting worse back in Fallon. Bummed out at first after receiving this news, my spirits rose back up when Scott said, "Want to try out the night vision?" and handed me some NVGs.

The guys marked targets with the laser out in the dark desert valley as I located them through the goggles. I took a little walk around, using the goggles as my guide between darkened patches of bushes. The sky was black and covered in a thick layer of clouds, but when I looked up with the goggles on, I could see the stars flickering like they had just been blown away. As I was raving about the technology, Andy mentioned I was lucky to be using it. He said many people are in the military for years and never get to use night vision at all.

~

I spent the next couple of days at Andy's house, where his whole family welcomed me right in. I talked with him for hours and enjoyed every last detail, no matter how small, that he was able to give me about his experiences in the military. Talking with Andy and Scott, I heard of friends lost in combat and small clues into missions they had been on. They had been all over the world. Seriously, both of them had been to five or six continents each. Much of what they had done in their careers they couldn't share with me, as their missions were often classified.
    I have always felt a heightened sense of appreciation for SEALs, mainly because they put their lives on the line in situations where they absolutely deserve praise, but almost nobody knows what they have done, simply because they wouldn't have a way to. The bits and pieces of information I did pick up from them, however, were intriguing. Like when Andy said, "Believe me, you know when you're getting shot at and it's a close miss. It's not like in the movies, when a bullet whizzes as it flies by your ear. It's more like a loud explosion next to your head." He even jokingly (I think) tried to recruit me into the SEALs, which I politely declined. My skinny frame wouldn't quite allow me to become one of the elite soldiers on the planet, I

didn't think. The training alone would likely kill me, except for maybe the long marches.

~

I did a lot of reflecting on The Loneliest Road during my few days at Andy's house. When I did leave Fallon, I'd be heading southwest to Carson City, while the official Loneliest Road route continued northwest toward Fernley.

What a road it was. Traveling so slowly up and over the pristine mountains and through the wide open basins was like therapy to me. The sunrises and sunsets, the dirt that caked onto my socks, the wind, the silence, the small towns and their resilient residents. It all drew me right in. After so many miles it truly felt like home.

Once Saturday rolled around, I made the short trip over to Scott's beautiful home for an end of summer party. I relaxed by the pool, made some new friends, and got to know Scott's family. The afternoon passed quickly as I spent hours drinking beer, talking, and eating far too many hot dogs.

Scott was solidly built and still an active-duty SEAL, the type of guy you would expect to have a tough demeanor. But as was true with Andy, Scott was as nice as people come. During one of our conversations toward the end of the party, Scott said, "Come on out to the truck with me, I have something for you."

We walked out into his home's driveway right around dusk. Scott opened his truck door and reached into the back seat, pulling out a small object from it.

"I want you to have this. I served as the commander of the Afghan Partnering Unit overseas, which meant that I was in charge of a group of both Afghan and

American soldiers. This was the medallion for the unit, not many of them were made, but I want you to have one. I think what you're doing is just great. You're really showing that you can do something if you put your mind to it," he said as he handed me a painted medallion a bit larger than a silver dollar and shook my hand.

Caught completely off guard by such a generous gift, I stuttered out as sincere a thank you as I could manage and nearly teared up while doing it. It meant so much. *Must not shed tears in front of a Navy SEAL*, I repeated to myself silently.

To add to the generous theme of the day, Andy gave me a shot glass made out of a brass 20 millimeter shell he had had shortened and polished himself. I would be leaving town with two new prized possessions.

After Scott and I returned to the party, I found myself wandering around aimlessly and feeling sad about the fact that I'd be leaving town in the morning. Fallon would be added to the long list of places I felt I left too soon.

What I didn't realize, however, was that the next interesting chapter of the walk would start before I even got a chance to leave the party.

After moping around for a bit, I casually struck up a conversation with an older man out by the pool. I can't remember exactly why or how we began talking, but once we did, I immediately knew I had made a great new friend. His name was Frank.

Frank appeared to be in his sixties, stood a bit over six feet tall, and had a wiry build. He wore glasses, but still squinted a bit to see things. He couldn't hear very well. I talked loudly so he could hear me, and he spoke loudly right back.

Being interested in my trip, he rattled off questions for a while. After filling him in on the journey, I asked, "What's your story, Frank?"

Chapter 25: You Control Everything

    Without much prodding at all on my part, Frank launched into his trying and fascinating personal history. At the moment he began talking, I had my iPod Touch in my hand, as I'd been using it prior to meeting Frank as I moved around the party. I had realized just seconds earlier that it had a voice recording application on it, which I was interested in testing out, especially in an environment where there were numerous conversations going on at once in close proximity. During this audio test I inadvertently ended up recording one of the greatest conversations I'd ever had in my life. I only remembered that it was still recording after our conversation was over. Dumb luck had once again prevailed.

    Frank began to answer my question. He said, "Well, I was married at 18, and then went off to Vietnam for the war. I got home from my deployment and my wife said to me, 'I love ya, but I just don't like ya anymore.' So I said *fuck that* and went right back over and stayed. After the war, I just started traveling. I'd be in Canada one day and Texas a couple of days later. I spent nine years living in my truck just traveling all over the place."

    I asked him more about his travels.

    "I've been through Europe, I've been to the pyramids. I've been all over. I've been throughout Asia, I've been to Australia, New Zealand. There are a lot of fucking adventures out there. Fucking life is amazing. You can learn, you can do, but when you quit, that's when life — *(shakes head)* — that 9 to 5 bullshit, DON'T QUIT!" he said emphatically, telling me to not stop traveling. "I'm losing my vision, so every night I sit out and watch the sunset. I could lose my vision anytime.

I've soaked up everything I can. My whole life's been that way," he added.

"I had some PTSD from being a combat vet. Was working as a bounty hunter at the time and ended up hurting a couple guys. The judge ordered me to go into the PTSD program, and the guy in there said that I had to learn the difference between hopes and expectations. I said that I didn't wanna hear that shit, but it's true. On expectations there are deadlines. With hopes there are no limits. You don't put limits on yourself. Don't put a lot of expectations on things, you set yourself up for fucking failure. You do, and you've got this pile of shit you're carrying around on your back, and you think your backpack's heavy? Motherfucker, let me tell ya, that son of a bitch gets so fucking heavy it's like carrying a diesel truck around, you know?" he said with a laugh. He then got serious and looked me dead in the eyes and said, "No one in this world can make you happier than you can."

Frank suffered from numerous injuries during his time in Vietnam, which would go on to plague his health for years. "I had pnemonia, then a relapse of malaria, and ended up in a coma for 2 1/2 months because of a stroke. I was *fuuuuucked* up. My right ear collapsed, so I still have a balance problem, and it changed my life. I spent a lot of time in a wheelchair. Major surgeries — three back surgeries, knees operated on, shoulders operated on, even diagnosed with a brain tumor when I was in the coma. When I woke up, they said it was inoperable, said I had six months to live. But a doctor told me about a new type of surgery. He said, 'You're a great candidate for laser surgery. Think about it, but you could die.' It ended up being successful, and here I am still today."

Frank and I ended up talking for about an hour. As the party wound down and I had to leave, Frank slipped a $20 bill into my hand. He smiled as he handed it to me and said, "Keep going."

~

As I was walking out of Fallon the following morning, a red truck pulled onto the dirt shoulder just ahead of me. The truck's window rolled down and Frank's face emerged from it. "Mind if I tag along for a bit and help you out?" he yelled out the window over the steady rumble of passing traffic. I told him he was welcome to join me for as long as he wanted to. He nodded in approval, then said he was going back to his house to grab some supplies and would catch up with me soon.

I continued on in the meantime. I passed a sign that read: PLEASE REPORT FOUL ODORS IN THIS AREA in bold letters with a phone number below the message. "You should call me in, Wilson," I said like a maniac.

Frank met up with me after a while. We were all geared up for a few days of adventure together. He was dead set on helping me out in whatever ways he could. For the next few days, that's exactly what Frank did. I walked during the days as usual, and at night we camped together and enjoyed one another's company.

While camping at Lahontan State Recreation Area just off Highway 50 on one of these nights, Frank went into more detail about his time in Vietnam. "In Vietnam, we went into an ambush. Not many of us survived. We were pinned down for three days. It was a rude awakening to life. Eighteen years old and you realize, ya know..." he said softly as he looked down, then continued, "Eventually I ended up in a POW camp. Me and two other guys decided to try an escape. We drew straws for the person who would have to distract them if they chased us. I didn't get the short straw. We went for it and the guy who got the short straw was gone pretty quickly. The other guy and me separated. I was still far from friendly lines, so for days I buried myself in the jungle during the daylight and moved at night. Sometimes the enemy would walk right over me without knowing it. I ate bugs for food, drank from puddles. Eventually I made it to a friendly camp. Boy, were they surprised to see me! I was a real mess."

He went on. "We'd be out there for months, taking fire every single day. The rain seemed to never stop, would just pour down all the time. We didn't have tents or anything, just slept in the rain. I started using a body bag to sleep in. I'd crawl in and zip it up to keep me out of the rain and keep the bugs off. People thought I was crazy, but it worked. When the rain would stop sometimes, I'd just sit there and think that it would be a good day to die. I always prayed that if I did die, it wouldn't be in the rain."

These were harrowing stories. Honestly though, they were some of the milder ones that Frank shared with me. After one particular story, which was grisly to the point that I actually felt sick to my stomach, I looked up to see that Frank's eyes were welling up. Mine followed suit.

I enjoyed spending time with Frank so much. His sense of humor was fantastic, his stories were remarkable, but the thing about him that I liked more than anything else was his appreciation for life. So few people truly realize how precious each day is. Frank had been to hell and back again, so he knew how fleeting every moment really was and the intensity with which he should treat each one he had left.

I walked a leisurely 20 miles the following day. Frank stopped every five miles along the road and waited for me to catch up to him for breaks. He set up his lawn chair right on the road shoulder and waited patiently for my arrival each time. During these breaks I ate, re-hydrated, talked to Frank, and smoked the hand-rolled cigarettes he always had ready for me. He tried to teach me how to roll my own, but I just couldn't pull it off. He rolled them in seconds with just a few swift movements of his old but nimble fingers. Frank and I stopped at a grocery store to pick up some steaks, potatoes, and beer for our last night of camping together.

Carson City was up next. Casinos, pawn shops, and bail bond businesses lined the main strip when we got there in the morning. While waiting for me in one of the city's many casino parking lots, Frank struck up a conversation with an elderly couple, who bought us both lunch once I caught up. After lunch at the casino I took a right on U.S. Route 395 and left Highway 50 for the last time. It felt wrong and unnatural, like I was leaving an old friend behind.

Frank insisted on getting a motel room for me in Carson City before he went back to Fallon. It didn't take long to hunt down a cheap room. We sat on a bench outside my room's open door puffing one last cigarette together before he departed. We passed it back and forth like old buddies. I thanked Frank for helping me out and being such an inspiration, as well as for sharing his stories with me. "Thanks for letting an old guy like me tag along," he said.

Frank got into his truck and left a few minutes later. I would miss every last thing about him. It was hard to watch as his old pickup jumped into gear and turned out of the motel parking lot. I'd once again be traveling solo, though I'd recently been finding myself growing more in favor of the opposite. But as many others had on the walk, Frank had imparted lessons on me that I would always carry forward, wherever I was going and regardless of whether or not he was actually there with me. Always conscious of the preciousness of life and the magic of the road, the last thing Frank said to me before leaving was: "Remember that there's no end to the adventures unless you put an end to them yourself. You control everything."

Chapter 26: Sierras

Not far from Carson City, I was set up to stay with the Dillwith family in Gardnerville. Lee and Jen Dillwith and their kids, Ella and Max, had graciously volunteered to take me in. They made my life way too easy for a few days. I only carried a small backpack during my daily hikes, while they took care of Wilson back at the house. I slept in a bed and showered every day. Jen and Lee made monstrous, delicious meals. Ella made me a milkshake every time I returned to the house from my walking. Max repeatedly kicked my ass at Mario Kart and let me stay in his room.

One morning after Jen dropped me off for the day, I saw something up ahead I had been waiting for quite a while to see. "That might be it up there!" I yelled out loud to Wilson as I approached a clump of roadside signs. The sun pounded down, sweat drenched my shirt and American flag bandana.

A blue sign with golden letters came into view.
Welcome To California.

I slowly made my way over to the sign and stood in front of it. I was emotionless. One of the moments I had tried not to think about for so long, yet one that still crept into my consciousness daily, had finally arrived. The last state. But there were no tears of joy, no yells, nothing. I had poured so much into the previous 3,000 miles that there seemed to be nothing left. I felt surprised at myself for being so dead inside, but didn't feel like thinking into it too much.

~

I decided to take California Route 88 up and over the Sierra Nevada mountains despite countless bits of advice not to. The road was well known for its narrow shoulders, fast traffic, and tight switchbacks. Something drew me to the mystery of the road less traveled, I guess, though it was clearly not a smart thing to do. The Appalachians were tough, the Rockies were no walk in the park, but they were both manageable. I got up and over both ranges without too much difficulty. But the Sierras were different. They were unforgiving and intimidating. Carson Pass would be where I could officially say I had conquered the Sierras, but I knew I was in for a good amount of struggle to get up there in one piece.

The California sun was relentless. While baking in it and dreaming of the cool mountain lakes and streams I hoped lied ahead, I saw a timely sign up the road that read: PARADISE LAKE - 2 MILES. This put a spring in my step, and I resolved to get there as quickly as possible. Upon closer examination about 50 yards later, however, I saw that the sign actually read: PASSING LANE - 2 MILES.

The uphill walking was endless. That's the only way I can describe how it felt. Endless to the point that I screamed at the top of my lungs in frustration about every minute. I cursed the skies that loved to downpour on me so often. I flailed a frustrated middle finger at the cars that nearly hit me by the dozens. Up, up, and up I went, with the only thing giving me any sort of respite from the torture being the stunning natural beauty that was everywhere I looked.

Breaks were frequent and required just to calm my frazzled nerves. I sat as quietly as possible whenever I indulged in them, just breathing in the smell of the fragrant fir trees and listening to the brisk wind blow through their branches above. The views were incredible. Looking back at Red Lake as I staggered up the final curve to the summit of Carson Pass was the only thing that kept me energized. A fine example of an alpine lake, its water glowed with a bluish-green hue. The sun ignited the lake, surrounding pines, and golden-brown grasses with the intensity that only California sunlight could. Looking forward, I saw patches of snowpack that hadn't yet melted away from the previous winter.

My walker senses picked up a fast moving vehicle coming up from behind me as I neared the Carson Pass summit. I turned my head to see that it was a California Highway Patrol car. The patrolman waved as he passed, then reached for his radio receiver. A blast of white noise rang out of his car's intercom, followed by a message of encouragement: YOU'RE DOING GREAT, MAN!

Finally, fueled by nothing but the sensation of being close to standing on what might as well have been the top of the world, I reached the summit. A sign read: Carson Pass Elev. 8574 Ft.

The excitement of topping the final range of the walk was promptly diminished when I realized the most dangerous and challenging part was still to come — getting down. Taking one last look at the summit sign, I continued deeper into Toiyabe National Forest with butterflies in my stomach.

~

The following couple of days of walking were probably the most dangerous of the walk. The slightest of driver errors would have been the end of me, and that is not an exaggeration at all. The road displayed the most extreme sort of S-curves, no shoulder, and many areas where metal guardrails took up the little space I *did* have to maneuver. On many of the hairpin turns, I was forced to the right side of the road because of a guardrail crowding the left shoulder. This usually meant I had to walk in the two feet of space available between the road and vertical cliff faces. Pinned between 2,000-pound vehicle projectiles and walls of hard granite, my life flashed before my eyes on several occasions. And those were just my concerns with the road and traffic. Bears and mountain lions roamed the surrounding alpine forest day and night. But despite the risks brought on by poor road conditions and the wild terrain and its creatures, the most dangerous part of traveling over the Sierras turned out to be middle-aged men on motorcycles.

During the weekend I spent up high on Route 88 before escaping to the much milder Sierra foothills, there were at least four separate motorcycle accidents that took place near where I was. On many of the road's sharp turns, bikers hugged the corners so closely that their handlebars and foot pegs came within mere inches of clipping Wilson. The bikes moved at speeds that were probably somewhere around double what they should have been. It seemed like there was some kind of contest going on over the weekend, which involved motorcyclists trying to do the dumbest shit possible and survive it. Not surprisingly, several people lost the contest.

While taking a routine roadside break toward the end of the weekend, a group of motorcycles drove by. The stream of riders that day had been constant, but one of the bikes in this specific group caught my eye. It was a red trike (three-wheeled motorcycle) with what appeared to be a husband and wife team of riders. The bike looked expensive and was neatly polished. I watched it fly by and cut tightly around a bend in the road ahead, disappearing from sight. They were going much too fast.

Less than an hour later, I rounded a corner and saw a line of police cars, ambulances, and fire trucks ahead. I approached the scene and asked the flagger who was controlling traffic what happened.

"Bike went off the road, husband and wife. Going way too fast," he said.

"Are they ok?" I asked, shaking my head.

He said, "Both of 'em," and gave me a thumbs-down sign with his hand.

Continuing along the line of law enforcement and rescue vehicles, off to my right I saw the bike that had flown off the road. The red trike I'd noticed earlier was flipped over and mangled. I had seen those poor people during their last minutes of life. I clearly didn't know them personally, but that didn't make it any less upsetting. The scene put a somber note on the rest of the day.

I finally began to feel the ambiance of approaching civilization as I wandered steadily downward. Traffic slowed down and scattered cabins and homes appeared, making the forest seem less impenetrable. The motorcycle traffic let up almost completely. I thought I was in the clear upon noticing these things, but as usual, I was dead wrong.

~

The sun was setting in the Sierra foothills, and I was stuck. I had inadvertently stumbled into a residential area. It came out of nowhere. One minute I was walking in secluded wilderness with cabins here and there, the next there were closely situated residences lining both sides of the road. Finding a place to hide Wilson and my tent for the night was proving to be a difficult task.

I called my brother, Ezra, to have him check if there were any campgrounds in the area for me, as my phone's Internet service wasn't working. Coming through as always, he told me there was a campground of some kind in Pine Grove, a small town ahead. The problem with this was I had no idea where I actually was. Pine Grove could have been two miles away or twelve. I hoped it was more like two and continued on blindly.

A deep darkness descended. It didn't take long before I was relying completely on my flashlight. There was nearly no road shoulder to speak of, so any car that came my way would force me completely off the road until it passed. Things were getting more dangerous by the minute.

Approaching the town of Pioneer, which I thought could have been Pine Grove, I stopped at a gas station to ask how close I was to the campground. It was a pretty simple piece of information to pick up, but the only person working at the gas station was a wrinkly old lady who was either insane or on drugs, or possibly both. I could tell immediately that she was unreliable. Hoping for the best, I asked her how far the campground was, despite the strong inkling that her advice may get me even more disoriented than I already was. She replied, "Oh, about two miles at the most. At the most. It's two miles at the most," repeating herself and fidgeting with everything she could get her hands on.

It turned out the crazy old lady conversion rate for distance was actually a multiple of four. I had no idea at the time, but Pine Grove was over eight miles away. Chugging an Arizona iced tea for a bit of hydration and a little sugar boost, I embarked on an eight mile walk that would end up feeling more like twenty or thirty.

About a mile from the gas station I spotted a shadowy opening to a narrow dirt road that led into the forest. Thinking it might finally be the option for a roadside campsite I'd been seeking for hours, I pulled a reluctant Wilson over a dirt embankment at the road's opening and took stock of my surroundings. There was a nice, flat piece of ground there. I surveyed everything with my dim flashlight. The spot was close to the road, but still hidden from sight by the embankment. It was perfect.

I grabbed my tent and began setting it up. As I did this, something crunched on the dry leaves and cracked a few twigs just out of sight in the shadows. I spun in the direction of the sounds. My flashlight flickered through the trees erratically, and I screamed like a little girl. Every shadow turned into a hunched over bear or a mountain lion on the verge of pouncing. There was no way I could spend the night in the forest full of shadow creatures. I had to get to that campground. Had a mountain lion not been hit and killed by a car just a mile ahead of me the previous day, I might not have been so on edge. What if that car hadn't killed that lion? Would it have then killed me? Is its vengeful mountain lion family looking to even the score? These thoughts rang around my head.

I threw my tent back into Wilson in an unorganized lump, and ran as fast as I could back to the road while dragging him behind me. At least the fear had given me a little jumpstart. I bounded up a hill and into downtown Pioneer. The problem with Pioneer was that it was not Pine Grove, where the campground was. It only had one motel, which was pretty far out of my price range. Looking back now, I would have just dropped the extra money had I known what was ahead.

Over the next couple of hours, I walked with as fast of a pace as I could manage, and even ran at certain times, all while still dodging oncoming traffic around fast turns in the darkness. Leaving Pioneer was a really stupid and dangerous idea. The sky was covered in clouds, which dimmed the normally bright moon and stars. The complete darkness engulfed me. I had to stop every few minutes to charge my wind-up flashlight, which only added to my frustration. I should have just quit, gotten over my irrational fear of the shadow forest, and set up camp. But the road had turned me into one seriously stubborn person. I was fucking pissed at this so-called campground for not being there. I couldn't be mad at myself, on the risk that I'd have a little roadside breakdown, so I had to be mad at something else. The campground was a convenient target. I had to show that campground who was boss by getting to it. I had to win.

As was the case during many occasions on the walk, just as I was about to reach my tipping point and roll into a ditch due to overwhelming exhaustion, I pushed up one final hill and saw a beacon of hope. This beacon was the elusive sign for the Gold Country Campground that my brother had told me about so many hours and miles earlier.

I stopped near the top of the hill, gazed up to the sky, and shouted, "Thank you!" to nobody in particular. The clouds had just cleared and the sky was putting on a dazzling light show. The moon was bright and illuminated the road to the point that my flashlight was no longer needed.

Turning left onto the campground road, I walked the remaining half a mile there without the interruption of a single vehicle. The campground office was closed, so I made my way past it, found an open tent site, and sleepily set up my home. I crawled into it on achy legs and collapsed in a heap, then quickly faded away from the exhaustion of a 35 mile day on the most treacherous stretch of pavement imaginable.

Chapter 27: Whiskey, Guns, and Gold

I awoke at around 10 AM the next morning and registered at the campground office for the previous night's late arrival, as well as for the oncoming evening. I figured I deserved a day off. By noon, however, I made up my mind that Gold Country Campground was where my solo adventure would end.

My mom was set to meet me in 12 days to provide me with car support to San Francisco, and I wasn't going to move a muscle until she arrived. It was odd realizing that the walk, as I currently knew it, was over. Adding to the somberness of that, I had lost my small American flag I'd been carrying every day since the beach in Delaware during the course of the previous night's walk. It sat somewhere in a ditch off 88.

While moping around my campsite and eating a late breakfast, I took in an emotionally charged bit of entertainment. A man, who apparently lived at the campground, was being arrested. He was resisting this arrest with as much vigor as he could muster. A pair of police officers wrestled him to the ground and threatened him with a taser. I watched the ordeal and giggled as I munched on my Pop Tarts. Just as the man was finally subdued and hauled off, I heard a voice from behind me.

"What the hell was that?"

I turned around to see a tall guy who looked to be in his late thirties. He was about 6' 4", had light reddish-blonde hair, and a big wad of chewing tobacco jutted out from his bottom lip.

"Some dude just got arrested, not sure why. Was pretty intense there for a few minutes," I said.

"Crazy, dude," he replied, "Did you get in late last night?"

"Yeah, really late. Walked in about 12:30 and just collapsed."

"You walked?"

"Yup, walking across the U.S., finishing in San Francisco, almost done."

He introduced himself as Brent. We talked for a few minutes and he said, "Well, come up to my site later today and we'll drink some whiskey and have a campfire." Being that whiskey and campfires are two of my favorite things, I told him I would definitely be there.

~

After enjoying a day of unbridled laziness, I made my way up to Brent's site in the early evening. His red Nissan truck was parked next to a wide family sized tent. The tent was practically the size of a small house. There was a metal trailer sitting unhitched next to it with a brand new four-wheeler on it.

"What are you doing up here?" I asked.

He said, "I'm looking for gold. Came all the way out here from Arkansas. It's been a dream of mine for quite a few years. I just saved up some money, bought the equipment, and here I am. Been here about a week so far. Found a few little flakes."

Brent made a campfire and we sat around for the next several hours eating, drinking whiskey, and sharing stories. As the whiskey consumption went up, so did the bizarreness of Brent's stories.

Among several other colorful descriptions of his experiences, I heard the tale of Brent's first experience in a Nevada brothel, with the slightly awkward highlight of the story being, "The first girl said I was too big, if you know what I mean, so I had to pick a different one. That made me pretty damn proud!"

Campfires, alcohol, and laughs have a way of creating a friendship in a matter of hours that would normally take weeks or months, so Brent and I were immediately pals. With an invitation to join him on an excursion into nearby Eldorado and Stanislaus National Forests for a couple of days, I threw my things into the back of Brent's truck and we were off the next morning.

The road into the camping area where we would be staying wound precariously up switchbacks, then back down into a deep valley along Moore Creek, a part of the north fork of the Mokelumne River. We drove through ghostly groves of fire damaged trees and hugged the mountain side of the road closely. Even the most unnoticeable driving mistake would have sent us hurtling down a steep face into a valley so deep and dense with tree life that nobody would be able to find us.

After the white-knuckle trip into the valley, we arrived at our camping spot, setting up just a few feet from the bubbling, clear river. The water rushed over moss covered rocks surrounded by patches of lily pads. We had enough food, booze, and ammunition for Brent's numerous guns to last us a few days.

We worked hard and played hard during our sunny days in the woods. Mining for gold proved to be no easy job. I stood in the cold river for hours, just digging buckets of dirt from the rocky bottom while Brent ran the material I dug up through a sluice box, then panned it down by hand in a gold pan. We took an excursion deep into the hills to look for an abandoned mine, but had no luck in finding it. In terms of gold, we found almost nothing, but it didn't really matter. As Brent said, "Gold is a fickle bitch."

Each night we had a campfire and swapped stories while drinking beer and whiskey. I carried a .357 revolver on my hip in a holster. Whiskey, guns, and gold. I was getting the true miner experience.

During one of these nights, as our fire died down and I was preparing to call it a day, Brent's inner pyromaniac kicked in out of nowhere. I could see a mischievous look in his eye and some sort of plan formulating in his head. This should have prompted me to stay awake and watch after my friend, but I was exceedingly drunk and decided to stumble over to my tent and leave him to his primal fire making urges. *What's the worst that can happen*, I wondered. Just as I zipped my tent shut and laid down, I heard an engine start. "What the hell are you doing?" I yelled as I poked my head out of my tent just in time to see Brent cruise out of the camping area on his four-wheeler. He vanished down a dirt road that lead far into the mountains. After watching Brent disappear into the darkness, I sat up worrying for about 15 minutes. I couldn't hear a sound. He had apparently gone out for a lengthy cruise in search of something.

I heard a faint engine rumble coming toward me just as I was getting ready to set off in search of him. After what seemed like several minutes of waiting, he finally emerged from the shadows. But something seemed different.

With one arm steering the four-wheeler, his other arm was dragging a 20+ foot long tree down the path that led into our camp. The tree was bulky and still had all of its branches still attached to it. I'm honestly not sure how he managed to hold onto the thing for so long.

I watched in silence as he staggered off the machine, lugged the tree over to the campfire, and attempted to throw the entire thing onto the flames. Shaking my head, but glad that he was at least not lost off in the dangerous Sierra Nevada darkness, I laid back down and soon dozed off again.

I awoke several times during the night to check on my friend. Curiously peering out of my tent, I saw Brent sitting at attention and monitoring his inferno from his log seat. I'd estimate that the flames reached six feet high or more at certain points. As each section of the tree burned down to coals, he dragged a new section onto the flames. The process was repeated over and over until the whole thing was eventually gone.

I crawled out of my home and walked past Brent's tent early in the morning. He hadn't bothered to zip it closed or even to get his full body inside it before passing out. His head was leaning out its door and a wide grin spread across his face. It made me smile to see him so content out there in the woods on his own little weird gold rush.

~

After a couple days in the woods, Brent and I were ready to return to the campground in Pine Grove. We were filthy, tired, and hungover.

Once we were set up again at the campground, Brent and I spent the next week setting out on day trips to dig buckets of what we hoped to be pay dirt, hung out at the campground, explored the nearby towns of Sutter Creek and Volcano, and took a drive back into the mountains, where the first snowfall of the year had already occurred. Standing on top of the Sierras and looking at the frosty, white blanket that covered everything, it became clear how fortunate I was to have gotten over the mountains when I had.

As Brent and I were cleaning our clothes at a laundromat in Sutter Creek one day, which is just a short drive from Pine Grove, he said, "Hey, remind me to tell you about the underwear story when we leave here."

"Ok," I replied with a laugh. Any story involving Brent and underwear would be entertaining, I already knew. About 30 minutes later, while driving back to the campground, I reminded him to tell me the story.

"Well," he began in his typical leisurely approach to a tale, "I used to date this girl, ok, and after we broke up I noticed she had left a pair of her underwear at my place. One day I ran out, all of mine were dirty, so I tried them on. Man, they were comfortable as hell! They were red with flowers on them or something. So I put them into the rotation."

"What do you mean? You wore them more than once?"

"Hell yeah, dude. I wore them for years after that. It was more out of a necessity than the fact that I wanted to at first, but they were great," he added and went back to focusing on the road.

Brent's ludicrous remarks only continued to entertain me more and more. At one point I told him I had gone for a swim in the campground's pool, so he asked me, "Did you piss in it?" When I told him that no, I had not urinated in the pool because I was an adult, he replied, "I piss in every pool I get in, every single one. I pissed in the Great Salt Lake. I piss everywhere, just to mark my territory." I made sure to not let him anywhere near the campground pool from then on.

While eating lunch at a local convenience store one afternoon, he said, "You know, man, I didn't know that you could go to a store and buy a sandwich until I was 15. One day a guy I was working for told me to get him a sandwich at a store, so I went to buy all the stuff — bread, cheese, meat, mustard. He said no, that you could just buy the sandwich already made. I had no idea! That's how backwoods it was where I grew up."

Because the weather was getting progressively colder every night, the helpful staff at the campground allowed Brent and I to move our things into a recreation hall on the property. According to Brent, it was "colder than a well diggers ass in Nebraska." There were a couple of couches in the building, along with as a dartboard, bathrooms, and best of all, heat. Brent, in his typically inquisitive assessment of his surroundings, sat down on a couch by the door and said, "Somebody banged on this couch. I can smell it."

For the next couple nights we sat around, drank beer, and watched movies. Kara, a very pretty girl who worked at the campground, joined us for much of this time, which I was thrilled about. Brent noticed and teased me incessantly about it.

~

After almost two weeks of hanging out together, the time came to say goodbye to Brent. It was tough to bid him farewell, as we had become close friends during the course of our adventures. I couldn't imagine what staying at the same campground for two weeks would have been like without him. I felt thankful for that miserable night hike that led me to Pine Grove so unexpectedly.

Brent was the exact sort of character I enjoyed meeting, mainly because I likely wouldn't have taken the time to get to know him before I hit the road. In what state of life other than wandering would I have gone into a dense forest with a foul mouthed, gun toting, whiskey drinking, brothel visiting stranger? My gut told me Brent was a lot like me — confused about everything, looking for something. We related on levels that just do not exist in a sedentary lifestyle.

    I said goodbye and wished him well on the long ride back to Arkansas. For all of his irreverent behavior and outrageous statements, Brent was as kind and caring as anyone I met on the walk. He shared things with me he hadn't told many people at all, and I did the same. I trusted him with my life on several occasions during our adventures and would do it all over again if the opportunity arose. I would miss our endless story swapping sessions, drunken nights, and his signature "Drop your cocks and grab your socks!" morning wake up calls.

Chapter 28: "He'd walk this road all the time."

A wave of excitement came over me as I walked through Pine Grove and into the nearby city of Jackson. It was where I'd be seeing my mom for the first time since she dropped me off at the other ocean, over 3,000 miles to the east.

When my mom arrived, she pulled into the parking lot I was waiting at, got out of her rental car, and hugged me so intensely that her glasses flew off her face and hit the ground. All smiles, it was a moment that gave me a hint of the magnitude of what I'd just done. The last time I'd seen my mom I was standing with my feet in the Atlantic Ocean. Now the Pacific was calling just ahead.

She had come to California early to be my car support driver, meaning she would be transporting me back and forth to my daily starting and ending points until I hit the ocean. My tent had been set up and taken down for the last time, Wilson was officially entering retirement. A tremendous sense of loss came over me on the drive to the hotel we would be staying at. I hadn't felt so sad since I'd left Alana back in Rangeley.

~

Wine country was up next. With the eased burden of just a small backpack and no longer having to maneuver Wilson around on narrow road shoulders, the walking was easy. I went past elegant wineries surrounded by sprawling vineyards. Their neat rows carved up the hillsides in every direction. The earthy smell of cultivated soil made its way to my nostrils from the surrounding hills and fields. The Sierras slowly disappeared behind me. I felt a knot in my stomach as they slipped further away with each step.

The days passed in a blur. I did my best to maintain my focus and take everything in, but as my elevation dropped further toward sea level, so did my spirits. I felt scared about the approaching end of the walk. A few friends would soon be arriving to walk the last couple of days to San Francisco with me though, which did help to alleviate some of the bad energy I had going on. For as much as the solitude of the journey had built me up, it had always been about people, and people were what would help me face whatever was waiting for me at that beach in San Francisco.

While approaching Point Reyes during my second-to-last day of walking, I stopped to check my directions at a dirt turnoff along the road, where I ended up striking up a conversation with a nice local lady who was also out for a walk. The road had a way of presenting perfectly timed occurrences, and this would be an important one.

After telling her I had just walked across the continent and was about to complete my trek, she said, "Do you know of a guy named John Francis?"

"Of course! He was the first real influence that got me thinking about doing this," I said. Francis had lived in Point Reyes for years, most notably when he gave up motorized transportation and began walking everywhere.

"He's an old friend. Moved out to the east coast now, but would see him often during the days when he first started walking. He'd walk this road all the time," she said.

I smiled and breathed deeply. The built up tension and stress I was feeling about finishing the walk instantly seemed less strong. It was the first time I thought about the ending of the journey as being a good thing. I'd read the article about John Francis' life in *Backpacker* three years earlier while sitting in my parent's living room, and there I was on a quiet California road, ocean practically in sight, with my very own story to tell.

~

    I took my last roadside break as a solo walker. My mom and friends were on the way to meet me. A neat row of pine trees lined the road. I took a seat beneath one of them in the shade it casted out. I leaned against the tree and thought about endings and beginnings, and knew I had to be open to both.
    I got back on my feet after a few minutes. The walk to the place where I was set to meet my mom and newly-arrived friends would be a short one, so I paid close attention to everything around me. I didn't want to miss anything. There was a tall hill along the side of the road. It sloped steadily downward, its side coated with golden wheat. I saw a large coyote, or possibly even a wolf, emerge out of the trees that topped the hill. The animal was muscular, rugged, wild, and sleek in its movements.
    The coyote made its way slowly down the wheat slope and sat down in the middle of it. It held its head high and sniffed the air, surveying the land to the west.

Chapter 29: Cold Water

My alarm went off early. The morning started like every other one had for the past week in the hotel. Get dressed, brush teeth, pack up, shoes on, grab breakfast, get to my starting point for the day, start walking. What was different about this particular day was that the end of it was the *actual end*. My walk across America would be complete by early afternoon.

After being dropped off in Sausalito, just a small handful of miles from where I would end the walk at Ocean Beach in San Francisco, I met up with the friends who would be joining me for the day. The short walk from there to the north end of the Golden Gate Bridge went by more quickly than I would have liked.

Approaching the east footpath that guides walkers over the bridge, I was caught off guard by a sign that said that no pedestrians were allowed on it. The east sidewalk was under construction, which left the west one as the only option. The problem with this was the west sidewalk was for bicycles only. You could wheel a bike across on foot while walking alongside it, but you couldn't just *walk* across it.

Deciding to go for it despite numerous warnings not to, my friends and I made it about a quarter of the way across the bridge on the west pathway before a Bridge Patrol car zoomed by, its uniformed driver yelling at us over an intercom to go back. Not wanting to make the day any more complicated than it needed to be, we turned around.

I called my friend, Sarah Peck, who was at the south end of the bridge, to tell her the situation. It's a good thing I have rebellious and motivated friends, because Sarah simply wouldn't take no for an answer. This is the same person who became one of the first two women (she went with a friend) to ever swim across San Francisco Bay from San Quentin to Alcatraz. Her level of determination when she sets her mind to something is almost inhuman. Sarah worked her way over the bridge patrol office, casually started a conversation with some officers, and convinced them that they should let us across. She called me back quickly, saying we were good to go. Sarah saved the day.

A few moments after beginning the bridge crossing for the second time, it became apparent that getting permission to cross was only one of the hurdles we would encounter. Over the thousands of miles of walking I'd done, I'd come to some pretty pointed opinions regarding bicyclists, which could all be boiled down to this — bicyclists are either the nicest people in the world or the biggest assholes in the world, without much middle ground to speak of. Unfortunately, it just so happened that the biggest assholes of them all were congregated in a whiny, spandex wearing mass on the Golden Gate Bridge that day.

People on bikes screamed at us and shot us dirty looks by the dozens. One guy rode by and yelled, "Wrong side, asshole!" and sped off. Several of them swerved at us on purpose, only to correct their paths just before impact and yell something they apparently thought would convince us of their superiority in the way of human powered transportation. It was the most pretentious sort of bullying you could imagine, a really embarrassing display of humanity. It took a lot of focus not to kick their wheels and watch them launch over the bridge guardrail into the bay below.

But moving along, aside from the obnoxious behavior of the yuppie bicyclists, the walking was actually quite pleasant over the bridge. I didn't quite know what to think as I progressed over the famed architecture below and above me. For so long I had done my best to not even think about San Francisco. But there it was. The wind blew hard, and my knees quivered each time I looked down thanks to my severe fear of heights. The sky was clear. Even with the persistent wind, the bay waters looked calm from so high up.

After getting over the bridge, we stepped onto a trail that we followed for a few miles. The path hugged the coastline closely. Up and down we went on the dirt trail, weaving through rocks and bushes. The water crashed onto the rocky shoreline. Ocean Beach, which sat just a few miles ahead, was closing in fast.

Looking back from the trail, the imposing structure of the bridge stuck out dramatically against the rocks, blue water, and partly cloudy sky. But it wasn't ugly. A structure as iconic as the Golden Gate Bridge becomes one with the natural landscape. Apart, both would be incomplete. I usually found the combination of steel, traffic, and natural beauty repulsive, but that wasn't the case there. The view was beautiful, if only for that moment and in that state of mind.

Eventually we ran into paved roads again and stepped through quiet neighborhoods. I became silent and walked without a word while contemplating all that had happened. I was so lost in thought that I didn't notice just how close we were getting to the end.

As we crested a small hill, a beach came into view just ahead. My heart began to pound in my chest.

Walking down a wide sidewalk with nothing but a concrete divider between the beach and myself, I found an opening in it and hopped down onto the sand.

I saw my mom, friends, Wilson. Without much emotion I took off my backpack, hugged my mom, and made my way toward the water.

My heart raced faster. I walked slowly just trying to take it all in. The air felt charged like lightning had just struck next to my head.

Then something soaked through my shoes. Cold water.

I kept going.

Bending down to touch my destination, the salty water rushed through my fingers. I kept walking once more, then stopped after a few seconds. My eyes welled up and everything hit me at once. The happiness, sadness of loss and sacrifice, frustration, and whatever other emotions I had picked up over the course of so many miles were finally released from the hold I had tried my best to stow them away in for so long. I had always known if I was to let them out at any time before that very moment, the results could have been disastrous. But it was really over. I could release it all, and out it all came.

Gazing out over the Pacific, the sun poked through the clouds and lit up the ocean in front of me. I couldn't believe it was real.

~

I'm really not sure how long I stood there in the water, but after some time I turned around and went back to my waiting family and friends. We relaxed together on the beach and watched the waves wash up on the shore. I hoped I wasn't being too awkward. It all felt stranger than I can even begin to explain. I was unsure of how to act. Joel, my friend who had bet me I couldn't walk 40 miles in a day, was there with the 40 beers he owed me for my longest day of walking way back in Colorado. I cracked open a couple of them right then and there. I called my dad and step-mom back in Maine to tell them I had made it. Everyone around me talked and laughed, but I was somewhere else — on a scorching highway in Kansas, under a bridge in Missouri surrounded by fireflies, eating biscuits and gravy in a grocery store with a bunch of old farmers, watching the moon rise over the silent desert, laying down in the wilderness while listening to the wind blow through the trees, getting charged by a ferocious bear in Colorado.

I thought back to my old life, the one I left behind for what I thought to be such a foolish adventure at the time. I thought back to the night I left Alana. It still brought a pang of regret. I saw myself collapsing on the side of the road in West Virginia and considering going home on that dreary day so many footsteps and miles earlier. I had never really understood why I always got up every morning and just kept going. Not one day of the trip did I *actually* know why I was there doing it. There were times when I thought that I knew, but really didn't. I just kind of kept going. I knew the walk had *something* good to teach me if I could just stick with it.

And I was right. On that beach I realized I'd always have the experiences I'd acquired on foot to cherish for the rest of my life, regardless of what they had cost me. Nobody could ever take them from me, and that counted for something. In fact, it counted for everything.

My thoughts were soon interrupted by the movement of those around me. Before I even knew it, it was time to go.

Walking away from the water I'd been walking toward for over 3,000 miles, I turned around for one last look over the Pacific. A swift breeze rushed up the beach and hit my face. A deep breath filled my lungs with fresh ocean air.

I saw Wilson sitting on the beach. It was time for our paths to split. We had toiled together and crossed the continent, but he wouldn't be traveling back east with me. It didn't seem right to just pack him into storage somewhere. I'd probably be continuing my adventures on the road soon enough, and it wouldn't be fair to keep him from doing the same. San Francisco was overflowing with people who could scoop him up and put him to good use. His wheels bowed and he was a bit torn up, but he still had a long life ahead of him.

Leaving him there was a strange and probably illegal thing to do, but it felt like the right move at the time. The whole walk had been one gigantic exercise in going with my gut, and my gut told me that Wilson needed to stay in San Francisco. Perhaps this was just one last official act of lunacy on a trip that had turned me into a crazy person. Either way, I simply did not give a shit. I had just walked across North America. Nobody could tell me what to do anymore. Or at least they couldn't until I got home, where I would run face-first into the real world once again.

HOME. I had never heard of a place so terrifying, so foreign. I would get on a plane and be there so undeniably soon. Once I boarded my flight back to the east coast, I would travel in roughly seven hours what it had taken me seven-and-a-half months to cover on foot.

Walking away from the beach, I caught one final glimpse of Wilson. The soft Pacific sand cradled him in all his lopsided glory. Anointed with holy oil in the mountains of Colorado, soaked with rain and abused by wind, carrier of life-giving water across barren deserts, conqueror of the Rockies, Nevadan summits, the Sierras

— he was a magnificent thing to behold in the California sunlight. I smiled as I looked at him — my comrade, my cheap-o baby stroller. That was the last time I ever saw Wilson. He looked happy.

~

I made it six weeks in Maine before the road summoned me back. I thought I'd make it longer. You would think adjusting back to a world of water that comes out of faucets whenever you want it, refrigerators full of foods other than granola bars and canned pasta, and beds guarded from the elements and animals would be easy. I certainly thought it would be, but it ended up posing a lot of challenges. Sure, in a lot of ways, home was joyous. I saw friends I had missed badly and reconnected with them. That was a beautiful thing. I enjoyed Thanksgiving with my family and knew I was in the right place, at least for that day.

But at the crossroads of living in comfort once again and reflecting on the walk's completion, I found myself dwelling on just how dangerous the trip had been. It is a peculiar thing to realize you should be dead. My nightmares were of trucks. Big ones. The same ones that almost turned my body to bits quite a few times. I could recall their roar as they missed me by inches. There were lots of cars sprinkled into my dreams too. The ones that swerved at me both purposely and accidentally. I woke up scared a lot. I laid in bed and clutched the pillow that used to be my little stuff sack full of my extra clothes and wished with all my might that home was the actual nightmare — that I could be back out there on the road and too busy with trying to make it from town to town to think about my mortality. I missed Wilson and my tent, like they could somehow protect me. I rolled out my sleeping bag on top of my bed's many blankets and slept inside it. I found some comfort there. Dirt from the Nevada desert that was still stuck in its deepest folds found its way between my toes. I vowed to never clean my sleeping bag. The backs of my forced-closed eyelids were screens of flashing faces, the characters I had found and grown to love across the American peoplescape.

I talked to Coulson a lot during these days. He finished his walk not long after I did. It was nice to have someone to talk to who could understand my struggles with adjusting. He freaked out and went to Belize to sit on a beach and try to get back to normal. I went to Colorado.

~

Denver, Colorado
Ten weeks after the end of the walk

Denver's mile-high air is causing me to shiver, but I like it. I lean into the Colfax Avenue cold. It reminds me of other times when I was cold on the walk thing. I'm tired of talking about the walk thing, but I still like thinking about it when I'm by myself. Everyone wants to know what kinds of lessons I learned from it and how it changed me. *Did you find yourself?* I found something, just not sure what it is. It seems like most people are not satisfied with the answers I have for them about the walk thing.

I'm walking to Tattered Cover, a bookstore. I arrive there and head to the travel section. As I stand in front of the big shelf of books looking for something to browse through, a father and his son approach it and stand next to me. The boy is young, maybe seven or eight years old. The father reaches for a book, and I recognize his selection. It is a book written by a woman about her walk around the world. I've read it recently.

"Great book," I say.

He nods at me, and then bends down to one knee in a fatherly way. He speaks to his boy at eye level. I stand there and listen. Fathers can be wise and I'm always looking for wisdom, even if it is eavesdropped.

The father holds the book up with both hands so his boy can see its cover clearly. "This lady walked around the whole world," he says. I steal a glance at the boy's face. His eyes light up with wonder, like he grasps the idea but can't quite fathom how such a thing could be possible. The father says, "Can you imagine walking like this, son, traveling so far on foot for so long? What an adventure that would be. Just imagine all the places you'd see and the people you'd meet."

~

Nate Damm is from Maine and has been living nomadically since February 2011. This is his first book. You can learn more about Nate and his writing at www.natedamm.com.